# Gardening: Tips From Garden Professionals

Created and designed
by the editorial staff of
ORTHO BOOKS

Editor
**Nancy Arbuckle**

Writers
**Steve and Suz Trusty**

Photographer
**Saxon Holt**

Designer
**Gary Hespenheide**

# Ortho Books

**Publisher**
Robert B. Loperena

**Editorial Director**
Christine Jordan

**Manufacturing Director**
Ernie S. Tasaki

**Managing Editors**
Robert J. Beckstrom
Michael D. Smith
Sally W. Smith

**Prepress Supervisor**
Linda M. Bouchard

**Editorial Assistants**
Joni Christiansen
Sally J. French

# Acknowledgments

**Consultant**
Ken Inouye

**Illustrator**
Pam Manley

**Photo Editor**
Judy Mason

**Editorial Coordinator**
Cass Dempsey

**Copyeditor**
Toni Murray

**Proofreader**
Alicia K. Eckley

**Indexer**
Trisha Feuerstein

**Color Separations by**
Color Tech Corp.

**Lithographed in the U.S.A. by**
Banta Company

**Additional Photographers**
Names of photographers are followed by the page numbers on which their work appears.
R = right, C = center, L = left, T = top, B = bottom.

Comstock/Michael Thompson: 3, 76, 77
G. Joyner: 74T
Michael Landis: 39
Peter Lindtner: 1, 81L, 84
Photo/NATS/Ann Reilly: 9, 32, 56, 89
Photo/NATS/Liz Ball: 3, 10–11
Photo/NATS/Jennifer Graylock: 60
Positive Images/John Bradley: 90T
Positive Images/Margaret Hensel: 63B
Positive Images/Jerry Howard: 3, 7T, 7B, 8, 18T,
   22–23, 34–35, 52, 54–55, 81R, 90B
Positive Images/Ivan Masser: 73

**Front Cover**
Top row, from left to right: You can "draw" landscaping ideas right in your yard; see page 15. Soak bare-root plants before planting to give them a fast start; see page 57. Tips for harvesting fruit appear on page 81. You can avoid weeding vegetables by using a mulch; see page 85.
Center row, left to right: Dozens of good ideas for growing vegetables start on page 77. You can rejuvenate a lawn with spot reseeding; see page 45. For the best display of bulbs, plant them in a single large hole; see page 62. Fill out a perennial bed with annuals; see page 62.
Bottom row, left to right: To keep your basement dry, slope soil away from foundations; see page 37. The professionals' hints for installing sod start on page 41. The fifth chapter, beginning on page 55, provides information on producing vigorous plant growth. Use plastic milk jugs to protect new seedlings; see page 69.

**Title Page**
Azaleas and bluebells blend in this professionally maintained garden. Garden professionals share their tips for keeping gardens looking great.

**Back Cover**
Surrounding a tree with a flower bed keeps lawn mowers from damaging it, and also prevents the lawn from competing with a young tree for food and water.

Address all inquiries to:
Ortho Books
Box 5006
San Ramon, CA 94583-0906

| 1 | 2 | 3 | 4 | 5 | 6 | 7 | 8 | 9 |
|---|---|---|---|---|---|---|---|---|
| 95 | 96 | 97 | 98 | 99 | 2000 | | | |

ISBN 0-89721-276-2
Library of Congress Catalog Card Number 94-67710

# THE SOLARIS GROUP
2527 Camino Ramon
San Ramon, CA 94583-0906

# Easy Gardening: Tips From Garden Professionals

# Meeting the Pros

*Through study and experiment, professionals in all areas of gardening have developed techniques for creating the very best results with the least expenditure of time and effort. Incorporating these techniques will increase your own gardening enjoyment.*

Like all pros, professional horticulturists have developed techniques for making jobs go better and faster. Most of these techniques evolved from many trials and errors or are the result of one individual's inspiration. Then, as workers change jobs or branch out on their own, the methods that work best are dispersed throughout the industry.

This book brings you the best of these techniques, presented as a series of tips pertaining to specific tasks. Each tip responds to a common question, problem, or need. Rather than looking to this book for instructions on completing a project from beginning to end, look to it for the kind of advice and information that planting supervisors, arboretum gardeners, golf course superintendents, arborists, or landscape contractors share with their crews to help them do a job quickly and effectively.

Each chapter contains tips from a different group of horticultural professionals: design specialists, tree care experts, turf specialists, nursery staff, and commercial fruit and vegetable growers. They break their material into broad topic areas, then into defined tasks, each of which contains a series of relevant tips.

When you are ready to begin a gardening project, skim through the chapter related to that task. Read the tips from the pros and you will complete the task more easily, efficiently, and enjoyably.

*Filoli Gardens, near San Francisco, demonstrates professional gardening expertise.*

## LEARNING ABOUT AREAS OF EXPERTISE

Horticultural professionals work in particular areas of specialization, learning how to design landscapes or to care for specific plant types—trees, turf, bedding plants, fruit trees, vegetables, or others. This section describes the work various professionals do.

### Design Specialists

Landscape design professionals fall into two major categories: landscape architects and landscape designers. Of the two, landscape architects generally have more formal training in design, and they must meet certain standards to gain certification in their field. They begin work on a project early in the planning stage and develop specifications for everything from earth movement to the design of the plantings.

Landscape designers often have a combination of design and plant care knowledge. There are landscape designers who have extensive formal training; others have skills that have been gained through experience. Certification is not required.

Both groups strive to create the most attractive arrangement of plants that meets the needs of the client. To complete their tasks successfully, design specialists first develop an understanding of how the client wishes to use the landscape. Then from that understanding they create the design. They must respect state and local ordinances and take into account the style of surrounding spaces, the climatic conditions, and the project budget.

*A landscape architect spends a great deal of time on the design phase of a project, ensuring the proper selection and placement of plants and, ultimately, the attractiveness and longevity of the landscape.*

### Tree Care Experts

Arborists, government foresters, tree surgeons, arboretum horticulturists, and tree service technicians all have hands-on experience caring for trees. Arborists, foresters, and arboretum horticulturists may sometimes have the opportunity to recommend tree varieties for a particular landscape. More often, they and other tree care experts work with existing plantings.

Tree care experts handle a range of tasks, many of which require specialized equipment and materials. They diagnose tree problems; apply control products; trim, prune, and transplant; and, if necessary, remove trees. Since trees are the largest, longest-lived plants in the landscape and usually represent a major investment of money and time, it is often advisable to contact one of these professionals when you need assistance with diagnosis and care. Then you can decide whether to have the expert do the work or do it yourself.

### Turf Specialists

A number of different professionals work with turf: golf course superintendents; estate managers; athletic field, park, and public-property turf-maintenance personnel; sod producers; and lawn service specialists. Their backgrounds and training vary widely.

Turf specialists work with many types of grasses and ground-cover plants. Their responsibilities include preparing the soil, establishing the plants, watering, fertilizing, diagnosing and treating problems, and rejuvenating any problem areas.

Turf is usually the largest portion of the landscape. This often makes turf care the most time-consuming portion of the home gardener's tasks. The turf professionals' tips in this book make lawn work easier and more efficient.

### Nursery Staff

The term *nursery staff* comprises many horticultural professionals: growers of field, container, and greenhouse plants; nursery and garden-center operators; conservatory horticulturists; certified nursery staff; extension personnel; master gardeners; public-property managers; and landscape designers.

Those on a nursery staff are more often generalists than specialists. Rather than concentrate their efforts on a specific plant type, they

*Top: Golf course managers must care for acres of turfgrass as well as mixed trees, shrubs, and flowers. Bottom: Arborists are expert at keeping trees, such as this crabapple, graceful and strong.*

work with a broad assortment of plants, throughout many stages of growth. They have a wide range of technical and practical expertise and an understanding of many subtle aspects of plants and plant care.

## Commercial Fruit and Vegetable Growers

Professionals who grow fruits and vegetables commercially include orchardists, truck gardeners, berry farmers, and pick-your-own operators, among others. They are all interested in the productive side of plant care: growing and harvesting fruits and vegetables.

Both technical training and practical experience are needed to grow fruits and vegetables commercially. Growers' expertise may be limited to a specific crop grown only locally, or it may cover the production of all vegetable, small-fruit, and orchard crops. Commercial growers frequently work closely with researchers, testing new varieties and experimenting with solutions to production problems. Sometimes the growers themselves

*A large and tasty harvest is the objective of commercial fruit and vegetable growers.*

develop and introduce new varieties and new techniques.

## LEARNING FROM THE PROS

Professionals in all these fields face the same obstacles as home gardeners, but because of the number of plants with which professionals deal, these obstacles are often greatly magnified. It is difficult to face the loss of one elegant elm tree, even more so to consider losing most of the majestic trees lining the streets of a city and filling its parks. An early frost that wipes out a dozen tomato plants for the home gardener can eliminate a season's revenue for a commercial grower.

Horticultural professionals spend much of their time developing cultural practices and preventive measures to keep plants thriving and thus less susceptible to problems. A healthy plant will withstand a minor insect infestation or even remain unaffected by diseases that infect surrounding, less healthy plants. A healthy plant can also better withstand short-term cold or heat stress.

The preventive tips provided by the professionals save overall maintenance time. An added step in soil preparation, an early pruning practice, or a change in watering technique may help to transform a struggling plant into a thriving one. The fruit and vegetable gardening tips will help you turn a small plot into a season-long production center.

Occasionally, problems will arise that call for major changes: a declining tree may need removal; badly damaged turf may need to be torn out and a new lawn established; changing surroundings and weather conditions may require a totally new approach to the landscape. The professionals have developed techniques to cope with such major problems. Their tips will help you determine the extent of the problem and the best means of solving it.

Whether growing a few flowers or caring for a fully developed landscape, the home gardener experiences a sense of accomplishment when plants flourish. Follow the techniques used by professionals to increase the productivity of your garden and to ensure success. Making a few small changes in technique may shave minutes from a project or end up saving hours by the end of the season. Following the tips contained in this book will mean less digging, mowing, pruning, weeding, and watering, leaving you more time to enjoy your plants and the beauty of your home landscape.

*Field plant growers are among the varied group of nursery professionals. Here, dahlias are being grown in huge quantities for sale.*

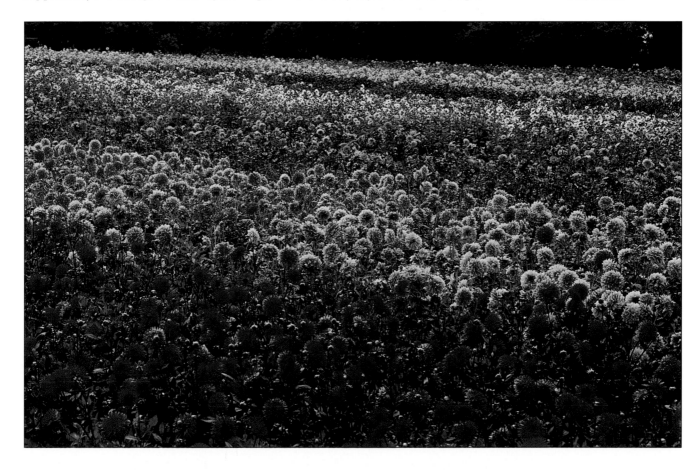

# Planning Before Planting

*Plant with a plan; it is much easier to make changes on paper than to an established landscape. Creating the dream landscape for changing life-styles calls for thinking ahead.*

A home garden is a gathering place, a learning and relaxation center, and a site for entertaining. Family members have different needs and different views on how space should be used. Landscape design can help you integrate these varying needs and functions into a plan for a workable and delightful landscape.

Landscape professionals—landscape architects and designers—deal with these issues. For commercial sites, the designer delivers the image the company wishes to project and provides a functional and pleasant workplace. For a home landscape, the designer creates the most attractive space compatible with the project budget, the surrounding environment, and the present and long-term wishes of family members.

Design techniques that landscape pros have developed work well for the home gardener. The right techniques can make any project easier or quicker and the results more pleasing, whether the project is adding a few shrubs, remodeling an overgrown section of the yard, or landscaping the bare lot of a newly built home.

This chapter contains tips on preliminary planning, accurate measuring, and deciding how to handle microclimates and prevailing winds. It offers information on plotting a design on paper and trying out different options on overlays. These tips make it easier to visualize a finished project, identify the traffic patterns of people and vehicles, make allowances for mature plants, and keep space open for long-range dreams. They also will help you avoid pitfalls and carry out tasks as smoothly as a professional.

*A well-planned garden takes into consideration site-specific features, such as slope and elevation, soil conditions, and climate, as well as family needs.*

## TAKING MEASUREMENTS

Developing a plan starts with accurately measuring and recording the lot boundaries and structures and any existing plants. All the elements of the landscape need to fit together like pieces of a puzzle.

**Use an existing plan**   Is there an existing plot plan of your home and yard? (A plot plan is also known as a site plan or deed map.) If so, use it instead of spending the time and effort to draw a plan from scratch.

**Photocopy the plan**   A clear photocopy of the plot plan can serve as the basis for the full landscape plan; use a copy to preserve the original. Check each photocopy against the original. Is there distortion? Distortion will be magnified in copies of copies. If you see distortion in the copy, discard it. Try to find the cause of the problem and correct it. You may have to use another photocopier. The copying process that creates blueprints provides the most exact duplicates.

**Update the plan**   On one copy, mark the locations of any existing plants or structures not already noted. These details can be transferred neatly to your final plan later.

**Team up**   Working with two people will save time in gathering measurements. One person takes notes while the other carries the end of the tape to different locations.

**Measure with a long tape**   A 50- or 100-foot tape makes it possible to measure long distances quickly. Cloth tape works best, especially for curves and angles.

**Use graph paper**   If you do not have a plot plan, draw shapes and record measurements on graph paper. Use a scale large enough to show all pertinent details clearly; for example, have ⅛ inch, ³⁄₁₆ inch, or ¼ inch equal 1 foot.

**Work in sections**   To make recording the details easier, divide the overall area being measured into sections small enough that their representations will fit on an 8½- × 11-inch sheet of paper. For example, you might divide the lot into the front yard, back yard, and side yard; into quarters (northeast, southeast, northwest, southwest); or into some other convenient unit.

**Use overlays**   To save space on the base plan, use overlays to record important garden elements—such as prevailing winds—that you need to consider in the design. To make overlays, cut pieces of tracing paper to fit over the base plan. (If your base plan consists of several sections, cut as many overlays as you will need for each section.) Use masking or drafting tape

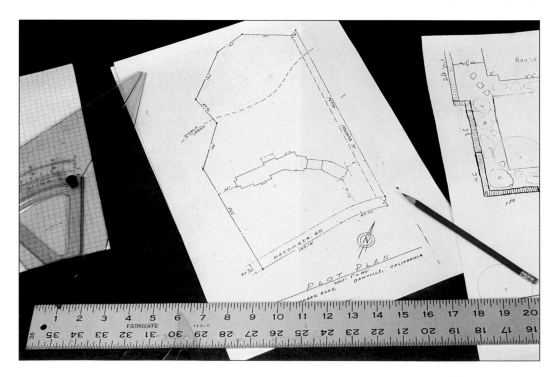

*To save time, start the design process with an existing plot plan.*

to secure each overlay to the base plan. Both kinds of tape can be removed later without tearing the paper (drafting tape comes off more easily). Overlays are also useful for sketching drafts of the design.

**Define locations accurately** Use a series of at least eight measurements to define the locations of major structures in relation to the legal boundaries of the property. To define the exact placement of the house or any other large structure, start close to one corner. Place one end of the tape measure against the side of the building and extend the other end straight to the facing property line. The tape should be perpendicular to the side of the building. Move around the corner. Take a second measurement from that side of the building, straight out to the property line facing it. Make two such measurements at each corner of the building. A straight line drawn through the two endpoints on each side will form the outline of the structure (see illustration at right). Once you have established the exact location of the house or another large structure, you have a fixed point from which to measure other locations. To accurately note locations, measure from at least two fixed points; three points are even better.

**Note climate characteristics** On overlays record key climate details: prevailing summer and winter winds, seasonally changing sun and shade patterns, and microclimates. (A microclimate could be a hot or cold spot, frost pocket, or other small area with a distinct climatic feature.) These details will be important later, when you are choosing plants.

**Note potential problems** Show the locations of easements, overhead wires, utility meters, air-conditioning units, outside faucets, downspouts, outside electrical outlets, dryer vents, and lighting fixtures. Mark the location and depth of buried electrical or communications cables; septic tanks; sewer, gas, or water lines; wells; and other obstacles to work around.

## CREATING A BASE PLAN

Recording all the details of existing structures and plantings provides a clear picture of the property—a picture you need before you begin to create the design. Use plants to complement

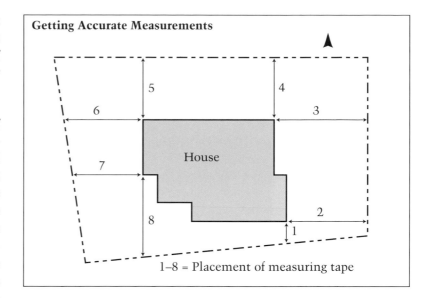

Getting Accurate Measurements

1–8 = Placement of measuring tape

the structures, to tie the structures to their setting, and to create beautiful yet practical living areas. By clarifying family wishes and needs and plotting different methods of realizing them, you can develop a workable plan to make good use of outdoor space.

**Gather drawing supplies before drawing** T squares make drawing straight lines easier. Use vellum (a durable paper) or tracing paper (either plain or with a printed grid) for the final draft if you intend to make a blueprint copy: Blueprint machines will not handle regular graph paper. Buy pencils with soft lead, designated as B or F, for rough sketches; use pencils with harder lead, such as H or 2H, for finer lines. Use an architect's scale to graph measurements without converting them. Transparent triangles that provide templates for 45-,

*Helpful supplies include a T square, a compass, drafting tape, an engineer's scale, clear triangles, a circle template, and several pencils of different colors.*

30-, and 60-degree angles make it easy to draw common shapes and angles. A compass can help draw any circle or section of a circle; a circle template is helpful for drawing individual plants and plant groupings. A white gum eraser helps wipe out pencil lines. Masking or drafting tape anchors overlays. Use different-colored pencils to identify details on sketches.

**Block out activity areas**   Tape a sheet of tracing paper over the completed base plan and draw free-form shapes (sometimes called bubbles) to block out spaces for various activities. Use different colors to designate private areas, public areas, and combination areas. Try out different patterns on additional sheets of tracing paper, overlapping and connecting the areas that are compatible and keeping separate the areas where activities would conflict or interfere with each other (see illustration below).

Use these bubbles to clarify your ideas about space requirements. Test the different arrangements to find practical, workable ways to get the most benefit from the outdoor living area.

**Double up overlays**   Place the overlay that shows climatic conditions on top of the overlay of activity bubbles to check for conflicts. Do the same with the overlay that shows elevation differences. Adjust the bubbles as necessary to match the activities to suitable locations.

**Use cutout modules**   When a certain feature begins appearing repeatedly in all the sketches, trace its outline on cardboard and cut it out. The cutout is called a module. Trace the module to save time, or simply move it around to work out design details.

**Develop blowups to show detail**   If an area of a sketch becomes too crowded, use a photocopier to enlarge that section of the drawing or translate the dimensions to a larger scale. For example, if ⅛ inch equaled 1 foot, try having ¼ inch equal 1 foot.

**Create living space**   Consider the landscape as an extension of family living areas. Develop a list of ideas about how the space should be used. The list should include input from all family members.

**Give sketched plans a trial run**   "Build" your landscape right where it will be by using temporary markers. Use flour, limestone, string, or garden hose to lay out the outlines of patios

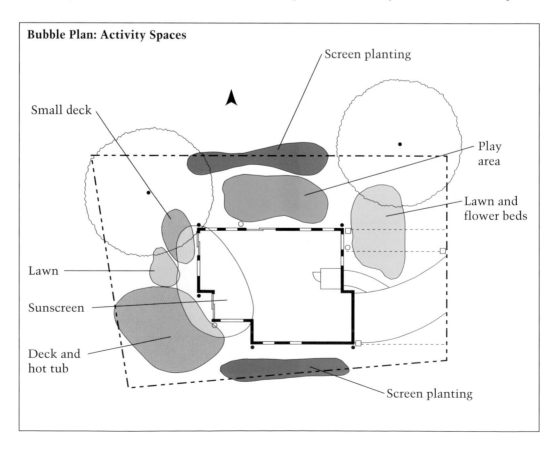

**Bubble Plan: Activity Spaces**

Screen planting

Small deck

Play area

Lawn and flower beds

Lawn

Sunscreen

Deck and hot tub

Screen planting

and decks, play areas, planting beds, or pools. Use sticks and boxes, balloons, or cardboard cutouts for trees, tall shrubs, and other upright features. Make fences and walls with blankets or sheets draped over ropes or string stretched between stakes of the proposed height. If a deck area is to be elevated, climb a stepladder to check the view from what will be sitting and standing heights after the deck is built. Also check the view from several angles.

**Avoid car shuffling**   Unless parking areas are carefully planned, multiple cars and different schedules can turn each departure into a car-moving marathon. Besides parking space for each car, you must allocate room for backing up, turning, opening doors, and picking up people and goods. Allow a minimum driveway width of 10 feet (12 feet is better), with 12 to 14 feet at corners and curves. Figure the space needed for turning.

**Screen unpleasant objects and views**   Plan to screen trash cans, recycling containers, compost bins, and undesired views beyond the property line. Use fences or evergreens so that the screening you choose will be effective the year around.

**Plan room for equipment**   Mowers and tractors will need access to all areas of turf. In fences and between structures, plan openings wide enough to allow easy passage of large equipment.

**Learn about building codes**   Before putting the final touches to the landscape plan, check with the local building department. Most structural remodeling and additions require a building permit and all aspects of design and construction must comply with applicable codes. Failing to obtain a permit may affect insurance coverage and even result in the demolition of the structure. Be sure to find out if existing easements will affect your design.

**Obtain cost estimates**   Before deciding on the specifics of a structural design, use concept drawings to compile a preliminary list of what you will need to complete the project. Check several sources for costs of a variety of materials that would serve the same purpose in the project. Modify the plan to use the materials that best serve your budget, the design, and your own taste. Draw up a new materials list, which incorporates the items you have chosen. Use the list to figure cost.

*Props help you visualize a sketched landscape. Here, a new patio is marked with flour, small trees or large shrubs with balloons, new flower beds with a garden hose, and a new wall with a sheet.*

## CREATING LIVABLE DESIGNS

In a successful design all elements of the landscape design work together to create the total look; each element complements and accents the others. With the broad variety of material and plant options available, it's possible to develop a beautiful, livable landscape to match any environment or budget.

**Select plants in stages**  During the early stages of developing the design, define plant options in broad terms, such as "Tall, slow-growing shade tree" or "Flowering shrub of medium height" or "Bed of brightly colored annuals." At this stage, select plants by their function in the landscape. List the features of ideal plants for each location. As the plan becomes more defined, narrow the range of choices until you are ready to decide on a specific plant.

**Select plants adapted to the local environment**  Choose plants that grow well in local conditions. Check plants already growing in the garden and ones in the neighborhood; determine which do best. Shop at local nurseries for improved varieties of native plants.

**Group plants that have the same basic needs**  Reduce plant maintenance and conserve water by grouping plants with the same general soil, nutrient, and water requirements.

**Plant to cut home energy costs**  Use plantings to modify wind direction. Channel summer winds and block icy winter blasts. Create shade for southern exposures; plant wind protection for the north and west.

Establish natural windbreaks perpendicular to prevailing winter winds. Protection extends for a distance one to three times the height of the barrier. Use curving sections of fencing or hedges to channel cool summer breezes to outdoor lounging spots or toward the house. Select trees with dense foliage to form heavy shade for cooling the house. Choose trees with lacy foliage to shade patios and decks.

**Cut maintenance time**  Before selecting plants decide how much time will be devoted to their care. Choose low-maintenance trees, shrubs, and ground covers if there's not too much time or energy for outdoor tasks. Expand patios and walkways to reduce areas of high-maintenance lawn and plant beds.

**Incorporate drip irrigation**  Drip irrigation systems are extremely efficient. They deliver a steady, measured stream of water directly to the root zone. The emitters, or drippers, available in many sizes, put out a certain amount of water each hour. The water flows from a central source, at low pressure, through flexible tubing. The system soaks only those areas immediately surrounding the emitters. Little water is lost to evaporation.

**Allow for growth**  Consider the mature heights and spreads of the plants; such planning now may save you from trimming, moving, or discarding them later. Space trees and shrubs at least one half their mature width away from structures. Choose plants whose mature size will be in scale with surrounding plantings and buildings.

**Pick plants for all seasons**  Select plants that will contribute beauty and interest the year around. Use a mix of evergreen and deciduous plants; vary bark and stem colors; choose trees and shrubs with twisting and arching branches. A carefully chosen selection will make a northern winter scene as lovely as the lush foliage and flowers of summer.

**Create illusions with color**  Use dark colors to define. Reinforce the strong line of a building foundation with deep green evergreens;

*Opposite: A landscape is seen and enjoyed from many different viewpoints. Plan for this in the design phase. Here, a front patio is almost hidden from the street (top). The walkway that leads to it (center) is both attractive and inviting. The patio makes a lovely view (bottom) from an upper window.*

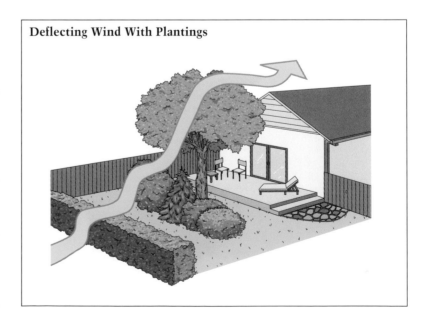

**Deflecting Wind With Plantings**

mark the edge of the property with a dense shade tree. Shorten distances with hot colors—bright red or orange roses planted along the back of the yard will appear closer than they actually are. Use cool colors to create a sense of distance—white or lavender roses by the property line will make it seem farther away. Enlarge small areas by using pale colors—plant soft pastel annuals along the edge of a small patio or in a courtyard to create the illusion of more space.

**Match textures to area size**   To accent and define the landscape design, mix the large leaves, heavy branches, and dense shapes of coarse plants with the lacy leaves and delicate branches of fine-textured plants. Select coarse-textured plants for large, open areas in distant plantings. Choose fine-textured plants to make small areas appear larger.

**Check the view**   The landscape will be seen by passersby, people arriving at the front door, and people sitting on the patio. Plan appealing views from each perspective. For example, stand on the sidewalk in front of your house and think what the entry will look like to visitors.

**Look from the inside out, too**   Plan for a pleasing view from windows and doors. If you don't want shade trees to interfere too much with the view, place them a minimum of 15 feet from the house and at an angle to the corners. Or place trees or large shrubs where they hide an objectionable view.

**Contain vigorous plants**   Use edging or fencing to keep fast-growing plants from overrunning neighbors' yards. Sink metal edging 6 to 8 inches into the ground to contain invasive grasses and perennials.

**Use accessories**   Accent the landscape with accessories that provide special interest, comfort, or enjoyment. Garden ornaments, statuary, folk art, and fountains—all add to the ambience of a landscape. Some garden ornaments make very strong statements and can alter the entire mood of a garden. For example, an old-fashioned gazing ball on a pedestal in the center of a flower bed or herb garden can add romance and mystery to a quiet garden.

*A birdbath, a tree, and some shrubbery make an appealing habitat for birds and other wild creatures. Their presence enlivens the garden.*

*Plants in containers bring color and variety to porches, decks, and patios.*

**Final Plan**

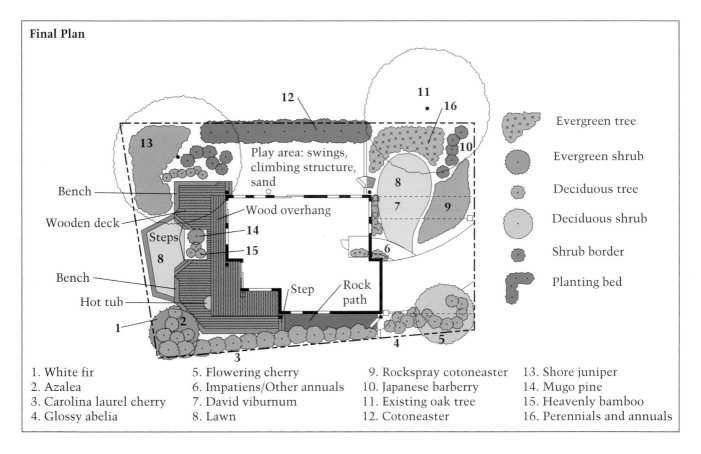

1. White fir
2. Azalea
3. Carolina laurel cherry
4. Glossy abelia
5. Flowering cherry
6. Impatiens/Other annuals
7. David viburnum
8. Lawn
9. Rockspray cotoneaster
10. Japanese barberry
11. Existing oak tree
12. Cotoneaster
13. Shore juniper
14. Mugo pine
15. Heavenly bamboo
16. Perennials and annuals

**Use containers to create portable beauty** Containers allow you to bring plants to soilless spots—patios, decks, and paved areas. Feature tropicals in sheltered locations. Choose large containers, or group many smaller ones, to achieve the desired effect. Hang containers of trailing plants for instant screening or to soften a background.

**Consider other creatures** Wild creatures need constant sources of food, water, and shelter. Plan assorted plantings that will supply them with fruits, berries, seeds, and nectar-producing flowers. Or set up feeding stations. Shade trees, evergreens, and other dense foliage offer sites for homes and places to hide. Plan a stream or pool or add a decorative birdbath to provide water.

**Light up the landscape** Add lighting to bring safety to stairs and pathways or to extend the playing time on a tennis court or in a pool. Some lighting options are easy to install, such as a self-contained solar-operated unit. Others require an electrician's assistance.

**Develop the final plan** Draw the final plan on tracing paper and then place it on top of the base plan. Double-check: Does it take into account the traffic patterns you identified, the best relationships between activity areas, and so on? Make any necessary adjustments, being accurate and concise and making lines and notations dark enough to see easily. Show all the details needed to bring the plan to life including the kind, size, and quantity of each plant and type of material. Use numbers within or beside the plant symbols to identify each type of plant. List the plant types with the necessary information about quantity and so on in a legend, or key. The legend should appear either on the final plan itself or on a separate sheet (see illustration above).

**Break the plan into blocks** Keep priorities firmly in mind and, considering both money and time, divide the project into workable blocks, such as a lawn, or a shrub border. Color-code the blocks to make it easier to see all the details. Follow a logical order of installation throughout, advancing from the rough work to the final touches.

**List all the needs for each phase** List quantities, sizes, varieties, colors, and all the other pertinent details about the plants, materials,

## Glossary of Landscape Design Terms

**Base plan**   Shows all existing details of property—legal boundaries, easements, structures, and landscaping. Gives correct placement and exact sizes. Used as a basis from which to develop a final landscape design.

**Blueprint**   A copy of the plan used by builders, architects, and landscape architects that lists details of property, buildings, and landscaping in white on a blue background. Created through a special process designed to keep information legible over long periods. The blueprint process can copy plans exactly, with no distortion.

**Deciduous plant**   A plant that sheds its leaves annually.

**Drawing to scale**   A method of showing a large area in a small space. Converts measurements to fit the drawing area while retaining the relative sizes of objects.

**Easement**   A right retained by a city, county, utility company, or other entity to use a portion of a property if such use is necessary.

**Evergreen plant**   A plant with foliage that remains green all year. May have broad leaves or needles.

**Frost pocket**   A low-lying or exposed area that is most likely to be affected by early- or late-season frosts.

**Microclimate**   A small area where, because of a combination of factors, climatic conditions differ from those of the surrounding climate.

**Plot plan/deed map/site plan**   Document showing legal boundaries of property, easements, and structures. Usually issued to buyer when property is purchased. Often used by contractor and builder to show construction details. May form the base map for a landscape design.

**Prevailing wind**   Most frequent wind direction during a specific season or time of day.

**Weep holes**   Small holes in a retaining wall that allow water to pass through rather than build up behind the wall.

and accessories. Make a separate list for each phase of the installation, and use these lists when shopping. Note the costs and availability of each item and whether any materials must be ordered in advance.

**Calculate the budget**   For initial estimates, figure what it will take to complete each step of the design. Then add half again as much to the money and time estimates as a cushion in case of unexpected expenses or adverse weather.

## FINE-TUNING THE LANDSCAPE

A few alterations to an installed landscape can make a pleasant area even more enjoyable and useful. Add to an existing patio area if it's being heavily used. Put up screens to hide unattractive views or to enclose an intimate space. Redirect traffic routes if necessary. Perhaps replant a slope to reduce mowing time. Before embarking on a project, consider the aesthet-ics of the new plan, the cost, and the effort it will require.

**Create screens to hide unpleasant views**   Hide views of telephone poles, shops, and eyesores with trees, fences, and hedges.

**Gauge effective screening heights**   Blocking an unpleasant view from seats on a patio may call for a 4- or 5-foot barrier; hiding trash cans and compost bins from view on a raised deck may call for 8- to 10-foot fencing or hedges or a vine-covered lath enclosure. To give a sense of distance to a small lot, keep the views as clear as possible. On large lots, break up broad open areas by using hedges or fencing to create outdoor "rooms."

**Plan double-duty hedges**   Select hedging plants that have showy seasonal flowers, fruit, or attractive fall foliage. Allow them sufficient room to develop into attractive, mature shrubs. Too little space often results in an unattractive hedge and extra trimming. Use plants with thorns to create effective barriers.

**Change traffic patterns**   Before attempting to change a traffic pattern, determine why it was established. Shortcuts worn in turf may be the best routes. Make the new route more attractive than the old one. It will be followed if it is quick, direct, connects frequently used areas, and avoids doors or gates.

**Create barriers**   Place plants to create barriers across undesired pathways and to separate the different functional areas of the landscape. A flower bed or low hedge may be enough to divert foot traffic. Use taller hedges to add a degree of privacy. Some ground covers are difficult to walk through and make effective barriers without seeming like barricades.

**Provide sufficient space**   For walkways for two persons walking side by side, plan a width of at least 4 feet. Provide 5 to 6 feet for greater comfort and ease. Allow extra width at curves and provide a gradual widening at the ends of the walkway for easy access and a gentle transition to surrounding areas.

**Lay stepping-stones**   Choose stepping-stones for paving little-used routes and creating pathways for leisurely garden strolls. Select stones with enough room for both feet, or place two small stones together or just slightly apart.

**Control erosion on slopes** Wildflowers or mixed ground covers can stabilize gradual slopes and save mowing time. On severe slopes, use diverse plantings: Interplant deep-rooted trees and shrubs with shallow-rooted grasses and annuals.

To stabilize the ground until the plants have developed, spread erosion-control fabric over the slope. Stake this heavy, coarse-weave burlap in place with wooden stakes and plant either seeds or plants right through it. The erosion-control fabric will rot away in a couple of years as the plants grow and begin to stabilize the slope themselves. Spread a mulch over the fabric if it is too unsightly.

**Design terrace strips** Stabilize and define a series of level, planted areas by using stabilizing materials between the levels. For heights of 4 feet or less, use walls of stacked rock, landscape timbers, or railroad ties. Place the first timber, railroad tie, or rock level at the base of the slope. Stack subsequent levels of materials slightly back from the preceding level. Grow plants in the crevices of the walls to stabilize the terraces and to add interest. If the terraces will be turfed, construct a ramp or access path for mowers. The path should be beside the stairway that serves the terraces or used in place of a stairway.

**Build retaining walls** For steep slopes that need support over 4 feet in height, build retaining walls. To keep water from building up behind a rock retaining wall and exerting pressure against it, place weep holes at frequent intervals. These holes will channel the water through the face of the wall. In low-lying spots or in areas of heavy rainfall, bury drainage tile along the base of the wall. To increase stability, insert concrete deadmen (3/8-inch iron rods anchored to concrete bases) at 3-foot intervals (see illustration at right).

If wood blends better with the landscape than concrete, use decay-resistant wooden bulkheads as the material in your retaining wall. Wooden retaining walls will eventually need to be reworked or replaced, however, since wood decays if constantly exposed.

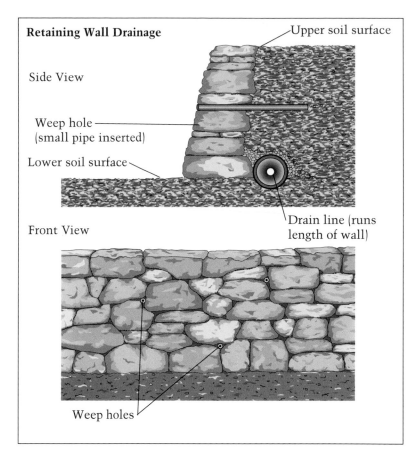

**Retaining Wall Drainage**

Side View

Upper soil surface

Weep hole (small pipe inserted)

Lower soil surface

Drain line (runs length of wall)

Front View

Weep holes

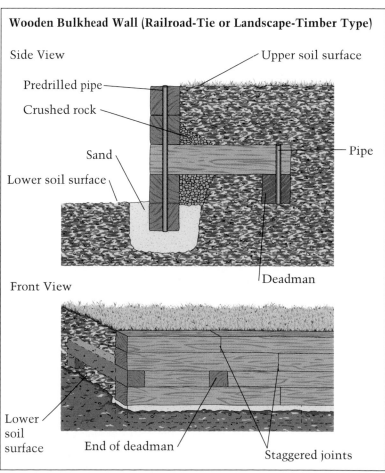

**Wooden Bulkhead Wall (Railroad-Tie or Landscape-Timber Type)**

Side View

Upper soil surface

Predrilled pipe

Crushed rock

Sand

Pipe

Lower soil surface

Deadman

Front View

Lower soil surface

End of deadman

Staggered joints

# Taking Care of Trees

*Trees dominate the landscape, setting the tone and affecting the environment of other plantings. Trees can outlive generations of humans. Because of their size, longevity, and value, trees require special attention.*

The value of trees in terms of their usefulness and beauty is hard to assess. Ancient civilizations cultivated trees to provide shade, screening against harsh weather, wood for building and fuel, fruit for consumption, and beauty and grace. Trees perform all these functions today.

Trees are the longest-living part of a landscape, nearly permanent features that outlast other vegetation, most structures, animals, and people. Trees are the most striking feature in a garden; their height and spreading branches and intricate and varied forms dominate the surroundings. Their sculptural elements shape the landscape more strongly than any other feature—sometime even more strongly than a house.

Although most of the time trees care for themselves with little help from us, they occasionally need human intervention to remain healthy. In addition, we intervene in their growth to train them to suit our needs. Proper training can make a tree stronger and more attractive than it would have been without training.

The professionals who specialize in tree care—arborists, government foresters, tree surgeons, arboretum horticulturists, and tree service technicians—have a broad range of information on the intricate mechanisms that govern tree growth. They have also learned a wide variety of techniques that ensure optimal tree care. The pros follow proper maintenance practices to provide trees with the best possible growing conditions and to prevent problems from occurring.

*The European beech tree gives a sense of timelessness, adding immeasurable value to this home.*

## WATERING

A tree is anchored in the soil by a network of roots that often extends two to four times beyond the spread of the branches. In most trees, 90 percent of the feeder roots are in the top 12 inches of soil. For water to be beneficial to trees, it has to be applied in sufficient quantity to areas where it can be absorbed.

**Make the best use of watering aids**   A variety of watering devices is available for watering trees: lawn sprinklers, drip systems, and spikes that feed water directly to the roots. Rather than water trees with the lawn sprinkler just because you already have one, select the device that best fits your situation.

**Watch trees for signs of water stress**   Wilting leaves and leaf scorching—light- or dark-brown areas between the veins or along leaf edges—often indicate a lack of water. When these symptoms appear, examine the entire tree. If the cause of the problem is lack of water, the wilting and scorching will appear first on new growth, spreading into older growth if left unchecked. If the lack of water persists, twigs and small branches may droop. In contrast, similar symptoms caused by nutrient deficiencies and disease organisms will usually show up on one section of the tree first, moving throughout a main branch, then spreading to other branches.

**Water young plantings often**   Mature trees may need only one or two waterings in midsummer; newer plantings may need watering much more frequently. Watch newly planted trees carefully.

**Test soil moisture**   To determine whether a tree needs water, insert a small-gauge pipe, wooden stick, or soil probe into the soil, to a depth of 12 to 18 inches, at four points spaced around the drip line of the tree. Moist soil will cling to the probe, dry soil will not. Move 3 feet closer to the tree trunk and repeat this procedure. Apply water where and when the probe comes out dry.

**Water evergreens the year around**   Deciduous trees use up to 40 percent more water than evergreens during the hot months. During winter months, however, evergreens continue to lose moisture from their foliage, so they need all-season watering.

Water all plantings before winter begins. During the cold months, water evergreens during warm spells, when the ground can absorb moisture.

**Apply water slowly**   Limit the flow from a garden hose to a slow trickle so that the soil absorbs the water. Start near the trunk—about one third of the distance from it to the drip line. Water at points 2 to 3 feet apart, in concentric circles 3 feet apart. Keep moving the hose until you have watered the entire root zone.

Alternatively, instead of a garden hose, use a sprinkler hose or a leaky hose, which releases water along its entire length. Place the perforated side of the sprinkler hose on the soil surface. A leaky hose releases water from all sides, so you can place it at any angle. Encircle the tree with the hose, starting close to the trunk, about one third of the distance from the trunk to the drip line. After that spot has received

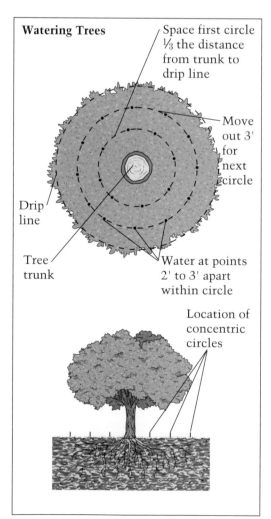

**Watering Trees**

Space first circle ⅓ the distance from trunk to drip line

Move out 3' for next circle

Drip line

Tree trunk

Water at points 2' to 3' apart within circle

Location of concentric circles

sufficient water, move the hose 3 feet closer to the drip line. Continue the procedure until you have watered the entire root zone.

Keep water pressure low and check frequently for runoff or puddles, especially when the soil surface is uneven, as on slopes or in rugged terrain. Use a soil probe to check that the area has received enough water before moving the hose to the next area (see page 24).

**Adjust turf irrigation systems to suit trees** Sprinkler systems designed to water turf do not meet the requirements of trees. Turf needs relatively frequent, shallow waterings; trees need infrequent, deep waterings. Grass roots are close to the soil surface and support only short, low-growing plants. Tree roots travel deep into the ground to provide for a much greater, high-growing plant surface.

In addition to growing deep, tree roots extend far from the trunk. In dry, thin soil, they may extend well beyond the limits of the foliage. Most of the feeder roots are well away from the trunk. Be sure to apply water over the entire root zone to water the tree thoroughly.

Use turf-type sprinklers or sprinkler systems for trees, if necessary, but avoid watering too lightly. A healthy tree may use two to three times as much water as a comparable area of turf, and a tree must have deep watering.

Place standard lawn sprinklers to cover only the root zone area, and keep the pressure low so that water doesn't shoot into the air. A portion of the water that sprays up will be lost to evaporation and wasted. Move the sprinklers to ensure that the whole root zone receives sufficient water.

**Install bubblers or drip systems** For an efficient, water-conserving system, replace traditional lawn sprinkler heads with bubblers, heads designed for trees. Install bubbler heads or convert to a drip irrigation system that is compatible with the turf irrigation system.

## ADDING FERTILIZER

The need a tree has for fertilizer varies according to the kind of tree it is, its rate of growth and overall health, weather conditions, and the pH and texture of the soil. Woodland trees feed on nutrients from material decaying on the forest floor; landscape trees usually need supplemental fertilizer.

**Use fertilizer to allow strong growth** Landscape trees may face a lack of nutrients from a number of causes: limited rooting space, competition from other vegetation, and poor soil structure caused by foot and vehicular traffic. Even the urban habit of collecting grass clippings deprives trees of nutrients that would normally be returned to the soil. Don't assume your trees will get nutrients from the lawn or flower beds.

**Time fertilizer applications for greatest effect** Apply fertilizer to coincide with periods of greatest tree growth. In-ground applications should begin in late winter or early spring, four to six weeks before bud break.

Spring-flowering trees will bloom better if they are given a light feeding in July, when they are setting buds for next spring's flowers.

In regions where temperatures drop below freezing for a major portion of the winter, cease fertilizer applications in late July. Later feeding may force new, tender growth that will be susceptible to damage from the cold.

**Apply fertilizer to the root zone** Apply fertilizer across the entire root zone of the tree, keeping 3 to 4 feet away from the trunk. When making surface applications, dry or liquid, follow the package directions to determine the amount you need; distribute it evenly. For

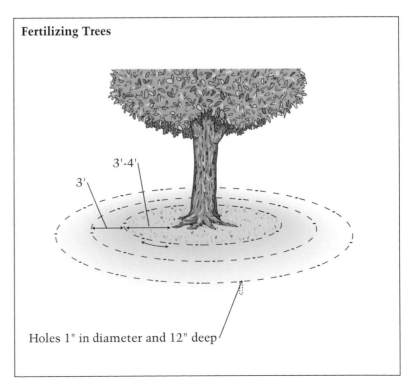

**Fertilizing Trees**

3'-4'

3'

Holes 1" in diameter and 12" deep

in-ground or below-surface applications, drill holes 1 inch in diameter, 12 inches deep, and 3 feet apart, in concentric rings spaced 3 feet apart. Alternatively, make the holes by driving tree spikes into the ground in this same pattern. Make enough holes to distribute evenly the amount of fertilizer recommended on the product label. Make the holes carefully to avoid causing root damage. If the drill or spike meets resistance, stop immediately and carefully start a new hole close by. Water slowly and thoroughly to carry the nutrients down to the feeder roots.

**Save time by using time-release fertilizers**   Time-release fertilizers are available in pellet, granule, and cartridge form, and as spikes that can be driven into the ground with a hammer. Some of these fertilizers release nutrients slowly for as long as two years.

**Give trees in lawns extra fertilizer**   Turfgrass, with its dense root system, is a tough competitor for trees growing in lawns. The grass absorbs nutrients before they reach the tree roots. Even though the lawn may be fertilized heavily, the tree roots under it may not be getting enough food to grow vigorously. Each spring, drill holes as described earlier and feed the tree below the level of the grass roots.

To further avoid competition, keep the lawn away from the trunk by placing a flower bed,

ground cover, or mulched area around the tree. This not only prevents competition for nutrients, but also protects the trunk from lawn mower damage.

## MAINTAINING TREES

To stand alone, without the protection of a sheltering forest, and attain desirable shapes, landscape trees require care. Early training usually produces the best results. Corrections made later take more time and effort.

**Prune evergreens**   Needled evergreens need little pruning to maintain their characteristic shapes, and many gardeners overlook the opportunity of pruning them. Prune evergreens to keep their size under control, repair any damage, and fine-tune their appearance.

**For a dense look, shear during flushes of growth**   If you like a hedge-like, sculptured look, shear evergreens in the spring. Some evergreens make one short flush of growth then, usually during a three-week period. Others continue to grow slowly throughout the warm months. The active growth periods are the time to shear them, cutting back the new growth at the ends of shoots.

One shearing per season may produce the desired dense effect. For rapid-growing varieties or to produce an especially compact form, two or three shearings may be needed. Several light clippings are better than one severe one. New growth will appear quickly from the side shoots, and new buds will form for next season, covering the sheared foliage.

**Trim pine candles before the needles unfold**   Prune pines while the candles, or new shoots, are still soft and before the needles have started to unfold along the length of the candles. Cut off one third to one half of the candle to form a fairly dense tree. To restrict the current year's growth severely, remove more—perhaps even the entire candle.

**Remove long growth tips of spruce**   During the early spring flush of growth on spruce, especially blue spruce, remove the long tip of new growth just at the point where the side shoots are forming. This will check outward growth for a season or two and encourage inner branches to fill in with new growth.

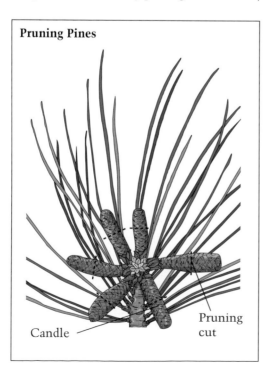

**Pruning Pines**

Candle

Pruning cut

*Left: Prune this branch just outside the ridge of trunk bark, without leaving a stub and without cutting into the trunk bark.*
*Right: This pruning wound is healing smoothly. An older healed wound is visible on the right side of the trunk.*

**Cut back yews**  Yews, and only yews, can be cut back drastically to spur new growth. Use this method to even the shape of plants that have been damaged, to rejuvenate old plants, or to resize plants that have become too large for their location. If you cut the branches of other conifers so there are no more needles remaining on the stub, the branch will die instead of sprout.

**Shape broadleaf evergreen trees when young**
Broadleaf evergreen trees rarely need pruning if they were trained to the desired form when young. Make cuts only as large as absolutely necessary. These trees close wounds slowly, and often don't ever completely seal large cuts.

**Prune deciduous trees to minimize wounds**
Trees don't heal wounds by growing new tissue, but by forming a barrier zone between the wound and the undamaged tissue. Plant cells called callus tissue form at the edges of the injury and may eventually spread over the barrier zone and close the wound from view.

Prune deciduous trees with two factors in mind. First, be guided by the natural growth pattern of the tree. Second, limit the size and number of cuts, thereby causing the least injury to the tree and reducing the amount of callus material the tree must produce.

**Prune without exposing trunk tissue**  Examine the point where a branch emerges from the trunk of a tree. A ridge above the branch, often called the branch-bark ridge, marks the point on the trunk. Beneath the branch is a similar raised ring of tissue. It is called the branch collar, or shoulder ring.

To prune back the branch, cut from a point just on the outward side of the branch-bark ridge to a point just on the outward side of the branch collar. This cut exposes only branch tissue and leaves neither a gash against the trunk nor an unattractive stub. When cutting, be careful not to damage the ridge or collar.

*Yew is one of the only evergreens that can be cut back sharply without killing the plant.*

**Remove misplaced branches**   Remove any branches that threaten to destroy the symmetry of the tree. Prune out crossover branches that grow toward the center of the tree, suckers that arise from its base, and watersprouts that grow vertically from limbs.

**Prune to promote compact growth**   Shorten branches throughout the canopy of a tree by pruning off no more than one third of their length. Cut just above a lateral bud. This forces new growth to shoot from along the branches, resulting in fuller foliage and effectively shortening the overall height of the tree. Nonselective topping—that is, cutting off the entire top portion of a tree at one time—will produce excessive, bunched new growth and destroy the shape of the tree.

**Time pruning to fit growth patterns**   Make any necessary large pruning cuts in late winter or early spring so that early-season growth will help to seal the cuts quickly. Prune to reshape the crown of a tree during the growing season, when poorly developed and diseased branches are most apparent. Avoid pruning in late summer, since it might force new growth that will not harden sufficiently before cold weather arrives. Remove dead, diseased, or dangerous branches at any time of year, as soon as you spot them.

**Prune in winter to stimulate growth**   To make a tree grow more vigorously, prune when it is dormant. Food stored in the roots and branches will be shared by fewer buds in the spring, and each branch will grow faster than if the tree hadn't been pruned. This stimulating effect can be achieved until new leaves begin to swell in the spring.

**Prune in summer to retard growth**   If you don't want a tree to grow quickly or if you are pruning a tree that produces suckers or watersprouts when pruned heavily, prune after the spring flush of growth has slowed. Pruning at this time has no stimulating effect, because the stored food has been depleted by spring growth. It's easier to see the effect of pruning when the tree is in leaf, but the branches are heavier and more difficult to dispose of than winter branches without leaves.

**Leave trunk shoots**   Allow small shoots on the trunks of deciduous trees to reach pencil size before removing them. These tiny side shoots provide nutrients to the tree.

**Stake trees only when necessary**   Although some trees require support, staked trees grow lankier and develop less sturdy trunks and smaller root systems than trees left unstaked. Trees develop thick trunks and strong roots in response to the stress of bending in the wind. If a tree stands on its own, don't stake it.

**Stake weak-trunked trees**   Tie the tree to its stakes as low as possible so the tree is able to move with the wind. Anchor support stakes for weak-trunked trees 6 inches above the lowest point at which the trunk can be bent toward the ground and still return to an upright position when released. Cut off stakes 2 inches above the anchor point so they won't damage the trunk by rubbing against it.

**Misplaced Branches**

Crossover branch

Watersprouts

Suckers

**Staking Trees**

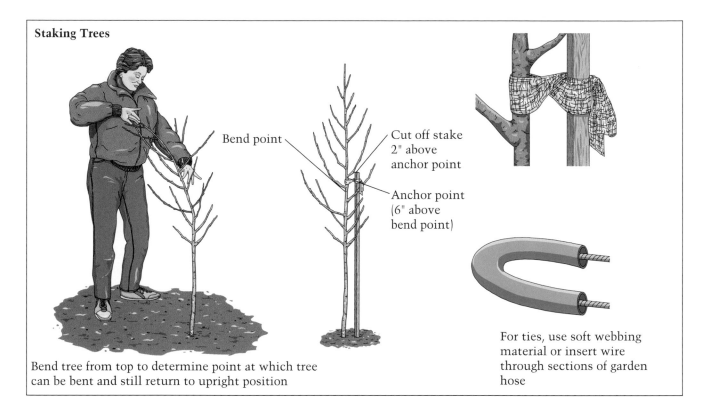

Bend point

Cut off stake 2" above anchor point

Anchor point (6" above bend point)

Bend tree from top to determine point at which tree can be bent and still return to upright position

For ties, use soft webbing material or insert wire through sections of garden hose

**Use padded ties**  Use soft webbing material or wires padded by sections of garden hose to tie trees between upright stakes. Secure the tie by making a figure eight—put the tie around the tree trunk and pass it back to the stake. This type of attachment allows the greatest flexibility.

**Position stakes to reduce wind damage** When using two support stakes, place them so that an imaginary line drawn between them is at a right angle to the direction of the wind.

**Choose the proper support**  Use one to three stakes to support trees up to 20 feet tall; use ground stakes and support wires for trees taller than 20 feet. Run hose-encircled wires from approximately halfway up the trunk to the ground stakes, placing the stakes so that the wire forms a 45-degree angle with the soil surface. Use one to four stakes, depending on the degree of support needed.

**Flag support wires**  Tie strips of bright cloth or plastic ribbon at regular intervals along the support wires. These flags will alert passersby and help to prevent accidents.

**Monitor the ties**  Tree trunks are frequently disfigured by wire or strong rubber ties cutting

**Ground Staking a Tree**

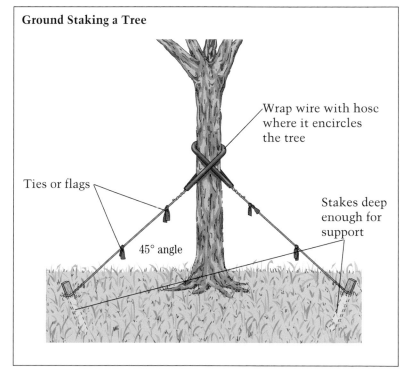

Wrap wire with hose where it encircles the tree

Ties or flags

Stakes deep enough for support

45° angle

into the bark as the trunk grows. Check the ties every few months to be sure they aren't marking the trunk.

**Remove the stakes as soon as possible**  The stake is a crutch, supporting the tree only as long as it is not able to support itself. Within a year or so, the trunk will have grown stout enough to support the tree without aid. Remove the stakes then.

## CORRECTING DAMAGE

Even with the best maintenance practices, trees may sometimes suffer damage. Many broken or uprooted trees can be saved. Assess the damage as soon as you notice it. If you're not sure if you should try to save a tree, ask a licensed arborist to check it and suggest appropriate treatment. Take the appropriate action and continue to monitor the condition of the tree for a while.

**Water roots and mist foliage-stripped trees**
Wind and hail can strip leaves from both young and mature trees, bruise twigs and sections of bark, and break small feeder roots. Yet as long as the branches are pliable and the tissue immediately under the bark is green, the tree is alive. Make a small scratch in the bark with a fingernail or knife tip to check for the green beneath the bark.

If the tree is alive, water the root zone adequately, but be careful not to overwater. With just a few leaves remaining, the tree will lose little moisture.

Two or three times each day, mist the upper portion of the tree with a fine spray from a hose-end sprayer or garden hose. Misting will encourage lateral buds to send out new growth. Continue misting until the new foliage is well formed or until the tree no longer shows signs of life.

**Reset uprooted trees**    Trees partially uprooted by high winds or flooding may sometimes be reset with good results. Dig out the soil where the roots were growing to make room for their return. The soil in the hole should be very moist—even muddy, if possible. To pull the tree upright, attach lines or cables to the upper trunk or use a block and tackle. During resetting, gently work the exposed roots into the moist soil. When the tree is settled, backfill soil to the original level. Anchor and prop the reset tree as necessary to support it until its roots take hold, which may be up to three years. Water the tree adequately, but don't overwater. Start adding fertilizer the second season after resetting.

**Prune to create a new leader**    When the growing tip, or leader, of a conifer has been damaged or when the tree sends out multiple shoots instead of a single leader, correct the situation with pruning. Choose the strongest shoot and clip off the others where they emerge. To create a new leader, make a fresh cut just above the nearest lateral (side) branch on the main stem. It may be necessary to help this shoot develop upright growth; encourage it to become the new leader by gently pointing it in the right direction and securing it with a soft tie. Pinch back any rapidly growing branches that may compete with it.

**Maintain tree form after damage**    Remove badly damaged branches, following the correct pruning procedures. Make a bottom cut first on heavy branches to avoid tearing bark along the trunk. Remove one or more other limbs, even if they are not damaged, to maintain the basic shape of the tree. When the damage is extensive, do remove the additional branches until the tree has recovered from the original stress. If the unbalanced shape does not increase the possibility of further injury, wait until the next regular pruning period.

**Creating a New Leader**

Prune here to remove damaged leader

Soft tie wrap

Wooden splint

Gently point and secure new leader in upright position

**Splint broken branches**  A broken branch can be repaired if the bark at the break is unbroken for at least one third the diameter of the trunk. Either prop the branch or use flexible bracing to return it to position and support it there. (Flexible bracing will be discussed later in this chapter.) Trim any ragged edges so the break will close tightly. Nail a board on one or both sides of the break as a splint to hold the break rigidly in place until new growth covers the broken area. Branches repaired this way will never be as strong as before. If the branch is very heavy or would be a danger if it fell, remove it rather than repair it.

**Trim torn branches**  Prune torn branches back to undamaged wood. This may mean trimming off an extensive portion of the branch or simply making a fresh cut slightly below the damaged section.

**Clean out damaged wood**  Insect attacks and disease may weaken sections of the tree and allow fungal organisms to enter and cause decay. Carefully remove the damaged branch portion, cutting well below the point of visible infestation. To prevent an infection from spreading, disinfect your tools after each cut, using a solution of 70 percent denatured ethyl alcohol or a 10-percent solution of chlorine bleach (1 part bleach to 9 parts water). Never prune when the foliage is wet.

**Install rigid bracing to support split branches**  Use threaded, rigid rods to reinforce weak or split branches on otherwise vigorous trees. Drill a hole all the way through the split branch; make the hole $\frac{1}{16}$ inch smaller than the rod. Insert the rod and secure it with washers and bolts. If necessary, use a wood chisel to clear a section of bark so that the washer fits flush against the wood. Use round washers and bolts; tree tissue closes around them more easily than around square hardware. For long splits, place a second support rod approximately 12 inches from the first. Stagger its position slightly.

**Use rods to reinforce weak crotches**  Use the same method to reinforce weak crotches as you would to brace a split branch. Crotches with angles that are narrow in relation to the trunk are not as strong as crotches at right

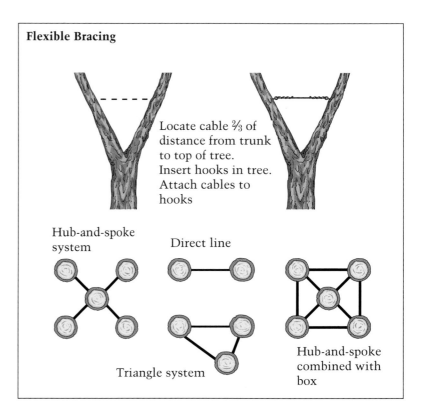

**Flexible Bracing**

Locate cable $\frac{2}{3}$ of distance from trunk to top of tree. Insert hooks in tree. Attach cables to hooks

Hub-and-spoke system

Direct line

Triangle system

Hub-and-spoke combined with box

angles to the trunk. The narrow crotches are in danger of splitting in a storm. Reinforce them by placing rods through the crotch.

**Use flexible bracing to support weak branches**  On an exposed site, storms or frequent strong winds may threaten to damage tree branches. Use wire cables that hook branch to branch to protect limbs high in the tree. Attach the cables to branches about two thirds of their length from the trunk. For maximum strength and flexibility, secure the cables so they are just firm: They should not be too tight or too slack.

The cables can be arranged in a variety of ways: between two branches; from branch to branch, in a box or triangle system; from a central branch in a hub-and-spoke formation; or by combining the box and hub-and-spoke systems. Place the cables high in the tree, about two thirds of the distance from the main crotch to the top of the tree.

Cable systems may need to be moved as the tree grows. Check their placement every six months. Fast-growing trees will require more frequent checks than slow-growing ones.

**Brace weak horizontal branches**  Install a cable-and-hook system to support an important, but weak, horizontal branch. The cable should run, at a 45-degree angle, from the branch to a higher point on the trunk. Attach the cable to hooks screwed directly into the wood of the branch and trunk.

**Install a prop when bracing is not feasible**
A desirable tree may lean to one side, placing pressure on the root system, or have heavy horizontal branches that need support but are not well placed for cabling. In these situations use a metal prop—a vertical one to support a branch, an angled one to support a leaning trunk. Insert a bolt through the branch and secure it to the prop to avoid exerting pressure on the bark. If extra support is needed, place props on a concrete base. Never anchor them in concrete; it restricts movement and limits flexibility.

In Japan, where old trees are admired and valued, props are often made into a decorative part of the landscape.

*The trees on this fine old estate lawn are protected by the planting beds that surround them.*

**Care for damaged trunks**    Trunk wounds can be caused by storms, nibbling animals, insects, vehicles, or trimming equipment. Most of the circulation through a tree occurs just under the bark. Wounds limit circulation of water and nutrients, slowing growth and weakening the tree. Wounds also allow the entrance of heart-rot fungi, which can eventually cause the death of the tree.

**Prevent mower and trimmer damage**    Damage to the base of the trunk restricts the flow of water and nutrients within the trunk and slows the growth of the tree. This injury is so common in lawn trees that arborists call it lawn mower blight. Keep mowing and trimming equipment away from tree trunks; lawn mower blades and string trimmers chip away or bruise bark. Look for obvious signs of damage, and treat any torn bark immediately. Internal damage may show as slowed growth on previously healthy trees or as a shrinking of bark tissue over the injured area. Monitor the growth of the tree; water and add fertilizer as appropriate.

**Treat bark injuries at once**    Inspect injuries to bark as soon as possible after they occur. There's a temptation to trim the damaged bark or shattered wood fibers, but that is not advisable. Instead, to keep the wound from drying out, refit the moist bark and wood splinters to the moist cambium of the exposed wood. Replacing even tiny sections will help. Tack the loose bark in place with tiny nails, and wrap the entire area with burlap or landscape fabric. Then cover the area with plastic and secure the plastic with cords. Remove the plastic after a few days, but leave the other covering. Water and feed the tree as appropriate, leaving the wound alone. After a year, remove the wrapping and carefully trim away any dead bark or wood splinters.

**Treat animal damage**    Check trees in early spring for damage caused by hungry animals. If the snow cover was heavy, mice and rabbits may have stripped bark from sections high on the trunk. Move areas of mulch to check for damage close to the ground. If possible, treat minor bark damage.

## PREVENTING INJURY
Although mature trees may appear invincible, they are living creatures and can be damaged. The culprits may be hazardous substances; lawn mowers, string trimmers, and other mechanical equipment; or harsh weather. Injury prevention is the best means of keeping trees strong and healthy.

**Use mulch and edging** Use a 3- to 4-inch-deep layer of mulch around the base of the tree, encircling it with a strip of edging to keep the mulch in place. Keep the mulch about 6 inches back from the trunk, to prevent insect and disease problems. The mulch will keep mowing and trimming equipment at a safe distance from the trunk.

**Use tree guards** To protect trunks from string trimmer damage, place a protective guard around the base of the tree.

**Place low fencing around trees in traffic areas** Trees close to sidewalks and driveways are targets for bruising and scuffing. Encircle the tree with a small wire or plastic fence placed a foot or two from the trunk.

**Plant a bed around the tree** A small flower bed, an area of ground cover, or some small shrubs planted around the base of a tree keep mowers and dogs away from the trunk.

**Protect trees from winter damage** Landscape trees rarely have the shelter provided by densely wooded forests. In addition, many landscape trees are not native to the region where they are growing and don't have the resources to escape winter damage. Give them a little help to withstand harsh winter weather.

•Soil heaving, caused by alternate periods of freezing and thawing, tears roots and can cause more damage to trees than cold weather alone. Place over the root zone of young and vulnerable trees a layer of organic mulch 3 to 4 inches deep. Keep the mulch 6 inches away from the trunks.

If heaving is severe in your area, wait until the ground freezes before applying the mulch. The mulch will keep the soil frozen through any early thaws, preventing it from refreezing.

•When possible, gently remove heavy snow from tree branches with a broom or bamboo rake. If temperatures rise sufficiently, spray ice-covered branches with water from a hose to speed thawing.

•Water during winter dry periods. Evergreens lose water during the winter as well as the summer. If the soil is dry, needle tips can dry and turn brown or needles can fall off. During dry periods when the ground isn't frozen, water slowly and deeply.

## Glossary of Tree Terms

**Callus tissue** The mass of plant cells that develops over cuts or wounds in trees on branches, sealing the exposed area.

**Canopy** The spreading branches and foliage of a plant.

**Drip line** The imaginary line formed under the outermost edge of the branches of a tree.

**Leader** The central or dominant stem of a tree.

**Pine candles** The tender growth tips of pines. New needles unfold from candles, which are named for their candlelike appearance.

**Root zone** The area in which active feeder roots are found. The root zone of a tree is normally the top 12 to 18 inches of the soil, starting approximately one third of the distance from the trunk to the drip line and extending as far as three or four times the spread of the branches.

**Sucker** A shoot that grows from the roots of a tree. Suckers usually arise near the trunk. If allowed to remain, they form a thicket.

**Watersprout** A vigorous shoot that grows vertically from a tree branch.

## DEALING WITH ROOT PROBLEMS

When trees grow freely in open areas, their roots develop fairly evenly around the trunk. In landscape situations, however, tree roots are often restricted by structures or by paved and compacted areas. Restrictions cause root problems that need to be corrected or adjusted.

**Remove girdling roots** Roots may wrap around the trunk of a tree, or girdle it. Girdling roots restrict the flow of nutrients. As the trunk grows, the roots cut into the trunk. Girdling roots can restrict the flow of water and nutrients through the trunk, and they can also constrict the trunk at that point, weakening it so it breaks off in a strong wind.

Use a chisel and mallet to break through the offending root at the point or points where it has attached itself to other roots. Sever several inches from each end of the cut root to keep it from reattaching. It is not necessary to remove the severed root section. Replace soil to its original level.

**Watch for unflared trunks** Where girdling roots are a problem, the trunk—rather than being flared where it meets the soil—may be absolutely perpendicular to the ground, so it looks like a telephone pole. Excavate soil carefully to avoid damage. Usually, the troublesome roots are within a few inches of the surface. Remove girdling roots as described earlier.

# Creating and Maintaining Turf

*Areas of turf tie together the total landscape and provide surfaces for recreation. The beauty and even the survival of turf are affected by how the home gardener uses and cares for it.*

Garden historians tell us that lawns evolved from pastures cropped by sheep or cattle. Today we feel that a landscape isn't complete without a "pasture" of smooth green grass around it. Although lawns are too thirsty for droughty Western climates and are more work—with their weekly mowing needs—than almost any other garden feature, we still love them. A lawn is the perfect foil for other garden features, the "canvas" on which we paint our natural landscape. It is the perfect play surface for children, and nothing feels so delicious to bare feet than a lawn.

Modern science proclaims the utility of turf. Grasses insulate the ground, keeping it warmer in winter, cooler in summer. The average front lawn has more than twice the cooling effect of the average home's central air-conditioning unit.

Grass protects against erosion, anchoring soil with its extensive and intricate root system. It absorbs water and prevents runoff, thereby replenishing groundwater supplies. Grass roots also purify water as it leaches through the soil to become part of the groundwater supply.

Turf absorbs atmospheric pollutants and releases oxygen—2,500 square feet of lawn releases enough oxygen to meet the needs of a family of four. Turf serves as a noise abatement system, working like acoustical matting.

But only in the Pacific Northwest does the Northern American climate favor lawns. Other areas are too hot during the summer, or too dry, or have the wrong type of soil. Over most of North America, having a perfect lawn calls for skill and experience.

Fortunately, turf professionals—university and extension turf specialists; sod and seed producers; golf course managers; estate managers; lawn service specialists; and athletic field, park, and public-property turf maintenance personnel—have provided home gardeners with improved types and varieties of grasses and better techniques for establishing and caring for them.

*Home gardeners can have flawless lawns by following the techniques practiced by turf professionals.*

## PREPARING THE SITE

Whether the site once supported thriving turf or is just bare soil surrounding a newly constructed house, the first step in creating an attractive lawn is to prepare the planting surface. Preparation techniques are basically the same whether the lawn will be seeded, sodded, plugged, sprigged, or stolonized.

**Prepare the soil**    A carefully prepared base for planting will make establishing a lawn much easier. Get rid of weed seeds, loosen the soil, add organic material and fertilizers, and your new lawn will get off to an energetic start.

**Remove existing vegetation**    Any weeds or weedy grasses on the site have well-established root systems. These plants will compete with the emerging turf seedlings for water and nutrients, making it hard for the tender young plants to survive. When desirable grasses make up less than 50 percent of the existing lawn, remove all vegetation and start fresh. (See Rejuvenating the Lawn, page 44, if 50 percent or more of the lawn area contains desired grasses.)

**Kill perennial weeds**    Kill perennial weeds with a weed killer containing glyphosate, which is absorbed throughout the plant, killing both tops and roots. This will prevent pieces of root left in the soil from re-sprouting and reinfesting the new lawn. Spray at a time when the weeds are actively growing, wait one week for the spray to be carried through the plant, then remove the weeds. Any pieces of root left in the soil are dead and won't re-sprout. Glyphosate breaks down in the soil in a week, so it's safe to plant the lawn as soon as the weeds are gone.

**Add organic amendments**    Most soils can be improved by adding humus-rich organic material, such as topsoil, composted manures, or composted yard wastes. Organic material harbors essential microorganisms, which help keep a lawn healthy. These microorganisms help to decompose sloughed-off tissues, make nutrients available to the growing plants, and improve soil aeration and water-holding capacity. Over the soil surface spread a layer of organic matter from 2 to 4 inches deep. Till this layer into the soil.

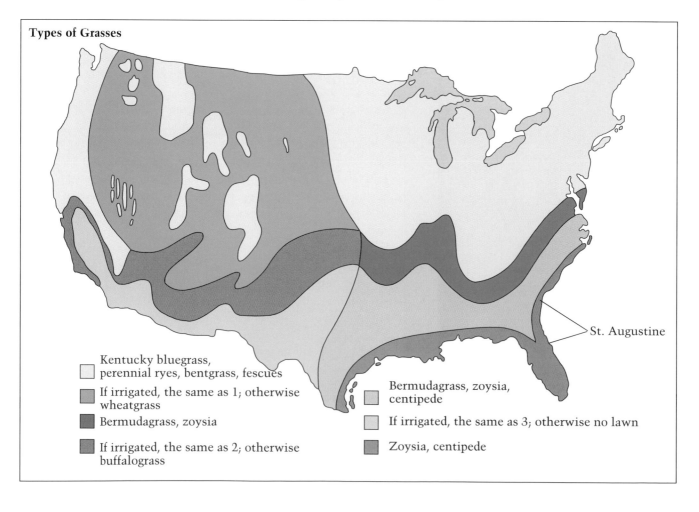

**Types of Grasses**

St. Augustine

Kentucky bluegrass, perennial ryes, bentgrass, fescues

If irrigated, the same as 1; otherwise wheatgrass

Bermudagrass, zoysia

If irrigated, the same as 2; otherwise buffalograss

Bermudagrass, zoysia, centipede

If irrigated, the same as 3; otherwise no lawn

Zoysia, centipede

**Add a complete fertilizer** Spread fertilizer with the organic matter. Both organic and synthetic fertilizers are available. Check the label for application rates. Use a rotary tiller to work both the fertilizer and the organic material into the soil to a depth of 6 inches.

**Water dry soil prior to tilling** Soil, especially clay soil, that has been watered a day or two before tilling will be softer and easier to till than dry soil. If your soil is heavy clay, water it three days before tilling to give it time to drain. Soil that is just moist—not too dry and not too wet—is easiest to till.

**Rake tilled soil** Use a rake to break up the clods of tilled soil. Remove as many of the rocks and as much of the other debris as possible. Rake the soil until the soil particles are about the size of sand grains or small pebbles. Too fine a texture turns the soil into mud when it's watered, and soil and seed wash away.

**Level soil surface** Tie a rope to the top rung of a ladder and another to the lowest rung. Tie the other ends of the ropes together to form one central pulling line at the middle of the ladder. Drag the ladder across the soil surface to level high spots and fill in depressions.

**Sprout weed seeds** If you are laying sod, it will smother most weed seeds. If you are seeding a new lawn, however, weed seeds can be troublesome. It's better to get rid of them before planting. Stop annual weeds by preparing the soil for the lawn, then watering it well to germinate the weed seeds. Spray the weed seedlings with an effective weed killer. Don't hoe or till them; stirring the soil will bring more weed seeds to the surface to germinate. Plant the lawn after the weeds are gone.

**Roll only if necessary** If the soil is not a clay type, use a light roller to help settle the soil evenly. Alternate rolling and watering until the soil remains level. Rolling helps draw moisture into the upper soil layers and eliminates air pockets, but it compacts some soils, making it hard for new seedlings to break through the surface. If your soil is a clay type (sticky when wet and hard when dry), avoid rolling. Rolling compresses this type of soil, squeezing the air from it.

**Slant soil away from foundations** If the general soil grade or depressed areas in the soil channel water runoff toward a building, create a 1- to 2-degree slant away from the foundation. Rake a small mound of soil against the foundation. Turn the rake tines up and gently drag soil from the mound to form a gradual incline that eases into the general soil grade. Smooth the soil surface and firm it with a roller, making sure to maintain the slant.

## SEEDING

Seeding allows you to choose the grass variety, but it's not always the best method of establishing turf. Not all varieties grow well from seed and the ones that do may not suit your area. (See the map on the opposite page for a general list of grasses that are most frequently used in each region.)

Seeding is best undertaken at the beginning of the ideal growing season: autumn or early spring for cool-season grasses, late spring for warm-season grasses. It is quick and easy to do, and initially the least expensive option for starting a lawn. However, a lawn started by seeding needs intensive follow-up care, including watering over a long period. It is slower to cover the area than other methods of establishing turf. Seed takes from 7 to 28 days to germinate; then the grass needs 6 to 10 weeks to get established before normal use.

**Select the best type of grass** Before buying seed, check with qualified turf professionals to determine which grasses are best suited to your area and the specific growing conditions of your yard. Once you have a short list, consider the water needs and time requirements for starting

*Channel water runoff away from buildings by forming a gradual incline from the foundation into the general soil grade.*

*Flags locate sprinklers in this newly seeded lawn. The sprinkler patterns have been adjusted to avoid the existing plants and trees, which have their own watering system.*

*As the grass germinates, you can see that the lawns have been kept away from the oak trees.*

and maintaining the lawn. Select regionally adapted cultivars that show resistance to common weather, disease, and insect problems.

**Apply seed with a spreader**    Tossing seed out by hand over anything more than a small area will result in clumps and bare spots. The more even the initial coverage, the faster the lawn will fill in. To apply seed evenly, use a drop spreader or a broadcast spreader. (See page 50 for tips on using a lawn spreader.)

**Embed the seed in the soil**    Turn a leaf rake so the tines point up and drag it lightly to cover the seed with no more than ⅛ inch of soil. Work the seed into the upper ½ inch of soil and roll with a light roller only if the soil is very dusty or sandy.

**Cover the seed with mulch**    Mulch the newly seeded area lightly enough to let light penetrate, yet heavily enough to protect the young plants from drying out. Scatter the mulch so that about half of the soil surface is covered with mulch, and half of the soil surface is visible through the mulch layer. Use sawdust or compost, or cover the area with an open-weave material, such as burlap or seeding mat.

**Protect seed on slopes**   Mulch newly seeded areas on slightly inclining slopes with a light covering of clean, weed-free straw. On slopes prone to erosion, cover the entire slope with strips of burlap, or seeding mat, running them horizontally across the slope. Pin this material to the soil with sticks or special landscape stakes available at garden centers.

Pay extra attention to watering slopes; the material and soil must stay moist, not soggy, from the time of seeding until the young plants are established. Water lightly and frequently.

**Water often**   After seeding, water the entire area well. Use a light spray, but soak the area thoroughly, applying approximately 1 inch of water. Then keep the area from drying out with frequent, lighter waterings—as many as four a day in hot, dry, windy weather. If you have a sprinkler system, use it cautiously until the ground is covered with grass. Most lawn sprinklers water heavily enough to float the grass seeds out of the soil and wash them into clumps. Water gently enough so no free water ever stands on the soil.

**Set out sprinklers**   Establish a network of sprinklers and hoses to water the area in the shortest time with the least rearranging. If you need to move the hoses, lift them. Dragging hoses will uproot the tender plants. Consider using timers to run the sprinklers once or twice during the day. Check the soil surface in the early morning and again in the evening; water as needed, even in the late evening.

**Adjust watering patterns**   Check the watering pattern daily, making adjustments if necessary to keep the soil evenly moist. Changes in air temperature, wind direction and velocity, and amount of sunlight will all affect water needs. Watch for puddling or soil washing away and prevent these problems by moving the sprinklers or adjusting the water flow.

**Take special care of the young grass**   Young turf needs special care until it is strong enough

to withstand normal everyday use. Water frequently, mow carefully with a sharp mower, and keep traffic off the lawn.

**Mow young grass**   Mow when the major portion of the new lawn has reached a height approximately one third taller than the recommended height for the grass variety. Check the chart on page 48 for general grass-length recommendations. If grass is normally kept at 1 inch, mow for the first time when the

*This broadcast spreader distributes seed more evenly than casting it by hand. Use this type of spreader for larger areas, and a drop spreader for smaller areas or more precise applications.*

seedlings reach between 1¼ and 1½ inches. As with any mowing, remove no more than one third of the blade at any one cutting. A reel mower is less likely to uproot new seedlings than a rotary mower. If you must use a rotary mower, sharpen the blade.

**Keep off**   Keep foot traffic to a minimum until the new turf is well established, usually not until after the third or fourth mowing.

**Remove weeds**   Pull or dig out weeds that extend above the lawn surface between mowings and whose aggressive growth is overtaking the young grass. Or spot-treat with a selective weed killer to remove broadleaf weeds.

## INSTALLING SOD

Sodding is the quickest way to establish a lawn and the most costly. Weigh the cost against the advantage of a nearly instant lawn (in most cases sod roots sufficiently to allow limited use within two weeks). The grass varieties available to you are limited to the ones the sod producers select, but they are normally those most adaptable to local conditions. As you choose a grass type and cultivar, carefully consider the water requirements and time commitment necessary for establishing and maintaining the lawn. You can lay sod successfully at any time of the year, but it is best to avoid hot and dry periods and to give the roots a chance to bond to the soil before harsh, northern winters arrive.

**Adjust the soil level**   Measure the thickness of the sod (it is usually about ¾ inch). Establish the soil grade so the sod will be just slightly below surrounding paved surfaces. This allows moisture to drain from paved areas easily and protects the sod roots from exposure and drying. Level the soil surface in the same way as if you were sowing seed (see page 37). The sod will conform to the shape of the underlying soil.

**Water the prepared soil**   A day or two before the sod is scheduled to arrive, thoroughly water the prepared soil. The soil surface should be moist when you lay the sod.

**Have sod delivered near the installation date**   Ask for the sod to be delivered very close to the day you're installing it. Sod that isn't planted quickly is vulnerable to yellowing from being rolled up or stacked and deprived of light.

**Examine the sod**   When it's delivered, the sod should be moist, green, and freshly harvested. More than a few discolored blades may indicate insect or disease problems. Yellowing, extremely long grass blades, and a tight mat of roots grown into themselves signal that the sod has not been cut short enough. Do not accept delivery of sod that is not up to standard.

**Minimize hauling**   Have the sod unloaded as close as possible to the lawn site. Sod is heavy; hauling it from the pallet to the lawn site may be the biggest part of the job.

If adequate help is on hand to lay the sod within a few hours of delivery, place stacks of sod at intervals along the perimeter of the lawn area. Sod is usually folded or rolled in strips 6 to 9 feet long and 18 to 24 inches wide. Check the dimensions of the strips before delivery so that you can calculate how many you'll need to cover the length of the lawn area; space the stacks accordingly.

If installing the sod will take an entire day or longer, place the loaded pallets in a cool, shaded spot. Check frequently to be sure the outside rolls do not dry out. Water them lightly if necessary, but be careful not to overwater. Soggy rolls may fall apart when moved.

**Remove rolls carefully**   Rolls of sod will be stacked with the open ends down or tightly wedged against the next roll. Sod strips may be slightly overlapped or interwoven along each level. (This keeps them from shifting during delivery.) Have the delivery person demonstrate the correct procedure for removing one roll without damaging the next one.

**Move sod to the site**   Use a wagon, yard cart, or wheelbarrow to move sod in small quantities from the pallet to the spot where you will lay it. If you cannot keep the cart on paved surfaces, spread boards to create a path so the wheels won't dig into the soil or newly laid sod.

**Preserve leftover sod**   Spread out leftover sod in a shady spot on any surface, even a driveway. Watered daily, it will live and stay in good shape for weeks. Use these sod sections to replace damaged strips or any that fail to grow.

*Sod should be moist, green, and fresh when it is delivered. Before accepting the delivery, check for any problems.*

*Unloading sod as close as possible to the lawn site will limit the time and effort involved in hauling it.*

*Spread granular fertilizer on the prepared soil before beginning to lay the sod. Lay the sod in straight lines, staggering the ends of the strips.*

### Laying Sod in a Yard With Curved Boundaries

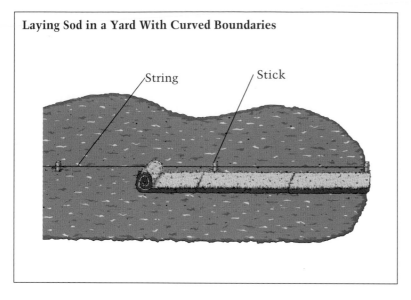

String     Stick

### Laying Sod Across Slopes

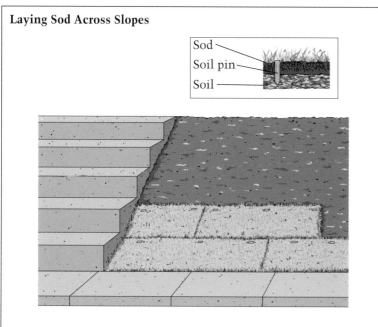

Sod
Soil pin
Soil

**Use plywood as a work surface** Work from a sheet of plywood laid on the prepared soil. Kneeling on the plywood will prevent knee prints in the soil, avoiding depressions and an uneven appearance in the new sod.

**Lay the sod in straight lines** Start laying sod along the straight edge of a drive or walkway. If the lawn is all curves, use sticks and string to mark a straight line down the middle of the area. Lay the first row of sod along this line.

**Stagger the ends of the sod strips** Place the next row flush against the previous one, starting the second strip at the middle of the first, creating a brickwork pattern.

**Use a knife** Cut the sod with a sharp, serrated bread knife. Lay sections so the ends just meet. Cut off any excess; don't overlap.

**Keep the sod tightly bunched** Avoid stretching the sod. It will gradually shrink back to its natural size, leaving small gaps. Instead, grab a handful of grass at the far end of the strip and pull it toward you, compressing the strip.

**Cover the spots where the sod segments meet** Fit sod seams together as tightly as possible. Use a trowel to slip soil or sand into the small spaces where sod segments meet, to keep these spots from drying out. Or pull back slightly on the sod ends, then add the soil. Tamp down the edges.

**Use large sod sections** Choose the largest sod segments available to fill in spots shorter than a full strip. Avoid small pieces; they dry out quickly.

**Lay the sod horizontally across slopes** Start at the base of a slope and lay a row of sod horizontally across the slope. To anchor the strips firmly in place, use three pins or stakes per strip, placed approximately 3 inches from the top edge. Fit the next row tightly against the first, moving up the slope.

**Roll the sod** Use a water-filled roller to press the roots into contact with the soil. Roll perpendicular to the length of the strips. To keep the air from drying out the roots in hot, dry weather, roll small sections soon after laying them, rather than waiting until you have laid all the sod.

After you have rolled the sod, rake it lightly to straighten any matted grass and hide the seams. Use a light touch so you don't dislodge the sod or pry the roots away from the soil.

**Water the sod daily** Newly laid sod needs frequent watering until it has bonded to the soil and is well established. Water sod deeply to encourage the roots to grow into the soil rather than around the rootball. Carefully lift up the corners of a few sod sections to be sure the soil underneath is moist.

**Mow young sod** Mow the new sod when it has reached a height slightly less than one third longer than the preferred length. (See page 48 for the recommended heights for various grass varieties.) Allowing new sod to get too long or keeping it too short will put unnecessary stress on the newly emerging roots.

Mow perpendicular to the length of the sod strips the first time you mow. The angle of the cut grass will help to mask any strip lines still visible in the lawn.

**Aerate to encourage growth**  Four to six months after installing the sod, aerate the soil to encourage water and air movement and strong rooting. Water the lawn two or three days before aeration; slightly moist soil is easier to work. Use a plug-type aerator (which removes small plugs of grass and earth) rather than a spike-type aerator (which pokes holes, compacting the soil in the process).

**Apply fertilizer after aeration**  The small openings created by the aerator allow fertilizer to filter down into the soil, to a depth where it is readily available to the grass roots. Apply the fertilizer, then water lightly to help wash it into the root zone.

## PLANTING WITH PLUGS, SPRIGS, OR STOLONS

Plugs, sprigs, and stolons are used primarily for starting warm-season and native grasses. (See the map on page 36 for regionally adapted grass varieties.) Warm-season grasses are best started in late spring or early summer, when they are actively growing. Start native grasses in early spring or late fall to coincide with their active growth periods.

Lawns established with sprigs or stolons usually take 8 to 10 weeks to cover the area. Plugs of the faster-growing warm-season grasses can produce a full cover in the same time span if you use 4-inch plugs and set them relatively close together. Plugs of slower-growing grasses, such as zoysia and Bermuda, will take approximately six months to completely fill in.

**Use the plugger properly**  To place plugs quickly and easily, choose a plugger with the same size and shape as the plugs. Plugs vary in diameter and may be round or square. Sink the plugger into the soil and then pull it straight up to remove a section of soil. Place the plugger back into the hole and drop a grass plug

through the top opening into the soil. Push down gently on the top of the grass plug while removing the plugger. Plugs may be inserted directly into the holes without using the plugger. This process is a little faster, but may damage the tender roots along the sides of the plug, especially in heavy soils. To check, insert one or two plugs directly, then remove them with the plugger and inspect them for damage.

**Space the plugs according to the desired coverage rate**  The closer together you place the plugs, the more quickly they will grow together to fill in the lawn. Space plugs no farther than 1 foot apart. Follow a crisscross or checkerboard pattern, setting the plant crowns $\frac{1}{8}$ inch above the soil line to encourage shoot development. Firm each plug into the hole by stepping down on it with the heel of a soft-soled shoe.

**Make furrows for sprigs**  Use a wedge-shaped hoe with a blade long enough to dig a 3-inch-deep furrow. Draw the first furrow parallel to the straight edge of a walk or drive; if there is no straight edge on the site, stretch

*Roots will emerge from sprigs, forming new plants. Place the sprigs in furrows, positioning them at a slant.*

*A stolon is an above-ground grass stem capable of forming new plants. Spread stolons across the soil surface and sift topsoil over them.*

string between sticks to establish a straight line. Draw the next furrow 1 foot from the first, and parallel to it.

**Place the sprigs in the furrows**   Place sprigs end to end along the entire length of the furrow, positioning them at a slant, with a small portion of the grass blade protruding from the furrow. Firm the soil around the sprigs with gentle pressure from the heel of a hand or foot. Start the second furrow 1 foot from the first. For faster progress, dig a second set of furrows perpendicular to the first furrows, and plant the sprigs in a checkerboard pattern across the yard. Planting sprigs in furrows takes longer than planting them with a rotary cultivator, but a higher percentage takes hold.

**Spread the sprigs over the soil surface and then till**   Tilling sprigs directly into the soil is the easy method. But compared to planting sprigs in furrows, a lower percentage of sprigs survive. Spread moist sprigs over slightly moist soil. With a rotary cultivator, till the soil in one direction to a depth of 1 to 2 inches. Use a light roller to smooth the surface.

**Top-dress stolons with soil**   Spread stolons across the soil surface. Place an open-weave wire mesh over them and sift topsoil onto them to form a covering 1 inch deep. Carefully lift the mesh and move it to the next section of stolons, then repeat the process.

**Keep the plants moist before setting them out**   Keep the young plant segments in plastic bags if you cannot set them out immediately. Use a fine spray from a hose or a trigger-type sprayer to lightly water the plants in the bag. The root systems must not dry out, yet overly wet conditions will cause decay.

**Keep plants on the soil surface moist**   Sprigs and stolons spread on the soil surface must be kept moist. If you are planting a large area or the weather is dry, work in small sections. Cover the stolons or till the sprigs under and then roll the ground before placing more on the soil surface.

**Water lightly after planting**   Use a gentle spray to wet the soil immediately after setting out the plants. Keep the soil surface moist to prevent the plants from drying out, and water heavily enough to encourage deep rooting. Check the soil moisture at the root level by digging into a few scattered spots with a trowel.

**Remove weeds**   Pull individual weeds as they appear or spot-treat with a selective broadleaf weed killer. Cultivate any weedy patches between the clumps of developing turf with a hoe or pronged cultivator.

**Mow tall weeds**   When there are too many aggressive weeds scattered among the developing grasses to make pulling them or hoeing them practicable, discourage them by mowing. Set the mower high—about 2 inches—to chop off the tall weeds. Several such mowings will weaken the weeds and allow the more vigorous grasses to crowd them out.

**Apply mulch**   Spread a light mulch of weed-free straw or sawdust to conserve moisture, repress weed growth, and temper the effects of harsh and erratic weather.

## REJUVENATING THE LAWN
When 50 percent or more of the lawn is filled with the desired grass, it is often better to renovate the lawn than to start over. The established grass can be stimulated to more vigorous growth and will protect the new seeds, sod, sprigs, plugs, or stolons.

To take advantage of natural growth cycles, renovate or revitalize a lawn of cool-season

*Spot reseeding will do much to rejuvenate a patchy lawn.*

grasses in fall and one with warm-season grasses in spring or summer.

**Kill unwanted grass**   Begin rejuvenation by spraying any areas of unwanted grass, or areas that are mostly weeds, with an herbicide containing glyphosate. Glyphosate will kill the grass and weeds, then break down in the soil so it won't interfere with the new lawn.

**Remove the dead turf**   Rent a turf-cutter to strip off the unwanted grass one week after spraying. It may not look dead yet, but it will not re-sprout.

**Replant the stripped areas**   Rake the surface of the soil to loosen it slightly, then plant sod, seed, sprigs, or plugs. Treat these areas as described for a new lawn on page 39.

**Overseeding warm-season grasses**   Since cool-season grasses thrive under the same conditions that slow the growth of warm-season grasses, attractive lawns of warm-season grasses can be maintained for a longer period by overseeding them with a cool-season grass. The cool-season grass provides color to the winter landscape and keeps weeds from developing. In spring the cool-season grass starts to decline and the warm-season grasses take over again.

**Reduce the grass height**   Lower the mower setting to cut the warm-season grass shorter than usual, which will improve air and water movement to the soil surface.

**Prepare for overseeding**   Remove the thatch so that there's clear soil for the seed. Then aerate the soil.

**Overseed when the grass declines**   As soon as the warm-season turf begins to decline, overseed with a fast-germinating cool-season grass, such as annual or perennial rye, or bluegrass. Check with garden-center personnel for the recommended variety and rate of seeding.

**Apply a light mulch layer**   Top-dress the seeded area with a light layer of mulch. Roll with a very light roller to ensure the seed makes good contact with the soil.

**Keep the seed moist**   Water frequently, but lightly until the cool-season grass is well established. Often late fall rains will supply a good share of the water that's needed. The cool temperatures and surrounding warm-season grass will help slow evaporation, which will further reduce the need for supplemental watering.

**Eliminate weeds**   Treat the lawn with a selective weed killer to rid it of broadleaf weeds. Use an herbicide containing 2,4-D to kill broadleaf weeds without harming the lawn grass. Spray the weedkiller over the entire lawn, or just where weeds are bad.

*Set the controls for speed and spike depth before beginning to aerate the lawn.*

the soil surface that stops weeds from growing through. Such controls must be applied before the weed seeds germinate. The controls generally last about six weeks. In most areas, an application in April or May is sufficient; in mild-winter areas, a second treatment in October will prevent cool-season weeds.

Since preemergence herbicides work by forming a barrier across the soil surface, any raking, power raking, aeration, or other procedures that disturb the soil surface should be done before application.

**Adjust mowing height**  When temperatures are high and natural rainfall less than adequate, allow grasses to grow longer than usual. Extra top growth helps to feed the plant and provides additional shade to cool the soil. Cooler soil loses less moisture to evaporation, making it more difficult for the weeds that thrive in hot, dry weather to take hold.

**Aerate the lawn**  Aeration opens up small holes in the turf and soil. A spike-type aerator has closed metal spikes that poke a series of holes in the thatch layer and underlying soil. A plug- or core-type aerator has open metal spikes that sink into the soil and pull out small sections or cores of soil, thatch, and grass. Plug- or core-type aerators are preferred in most situations because they do not compact the soil the way spike-type aerators do.

The holes created by aeration help open up compacted soils and heavy thatch layers. Through these holes water, nutrients, and air pass easily into the soil and to the grass roots. Grasses extend their roots into the openings.

Even healthy, thriving lawns benefit from aeration once or twice a year. Stressed lawns, in need of rejuvenation, should be aerated as often as once a month.

**Spot-treat frequently**  Treat new weeds as soon as they appear. This way they will never go to seed, and you will have fewer weeds every season. Walk the entire lawn every couple of weeks, spraying any weeds you see. Aerosol cans or trigger sprayers set to spray a fine stream are most convenient. Keep a can of herbicide containing 2,4-D in one hand—use this product for broadleaf weeds like dandelion. Outfit the other hand with an herbicide containing glyphosate. The glyphosate will kill lawn grasses, so spray it carefully. Use it on weedy grasses, such as crabgrass or tall fescue, that are crowding out lawn grasses.

**Apply preemergence controls**  Annual grassy weeds complete their life cycle in a single year, producing and dropping seeds that emerge the next year. These weeds are susceptible to preemergence controls, which form a barrier on

**Select an appropriate aerator**  Small hand-held aerators with a step-on base are available at retail outlets. These aerators remove two plugs at each step. They are useful for treating small areas or for frequently aerating pathways and other highly compacted spots.

Walk-behind power aerators may be rented at equipment rental agencies and many nurseries and garden centers. Most power aerators have controls for speed and spike depth. Before renting power equipment, measure the

CREATING AND MAINTAINING TURF

widths of any limiting features in the landscape—gate widths, the space between the garage and fence and so on. Make sure the machine you rent can get to the lawn. Operating walk-behind units is a time-consuming and vigorous task. Consider hiring a lawn care professional to handle aeration.

**Water the lawn well**  A lawn watered well several days before aeration is easier on the equipment and the operator than a dry lawn. When aerating, be careful not to damage lawn sprinklers.

**Leave cores on the surface**  Aeration pulls out cores of earth and leaves them on the soil surface. In most cases, it is fine to leave the cores there. They normally disintegrate in 7 to 10 days, adding organic matter to the lawn. If you prefer, you can rake up the plugs and add them to the compost pile or work them into other garden areas.

**Minimize thatch**  Thatch—a buildup of organic debris—sits above the soil surface and below the grass blades. When thatch buildup reaches ½ inch or more, it restricts the movement of water, oxygen, fertilizer, and chemical treatments. Grass roots may grow upward into the thatch instead of deep into the soil. Thatch can also harbor insects and disease organisms. To attain a lawn with minimal thatch, you must use the appropriate tools to remove it, and prevent it from accumulating again.

•To check the thatch level, remove cores of turf and soil from several sections of the lawn, making three cuts with a knife, as you would plug a watermelon. Or you can use a trowel, shovel, or bulb planter. The layer of material between the soil surface and the grass blades is the thatch. If this layer is thicker than ½ inch, it needs to be removed.

•To remove excess thatch, use a power rake or vertical cutter. Power rakes have a combination of springs and narrow steel tines that cut into the thatch layer. Vertical cutters, also called vertical mowers, have vertical metal blades to slice into the thatch layer. Both are powered by gasoline engines and are available for rental at many nurseries and garden centers and equipment rental outlets. Before renting, measure the machine to be sure it will fit into all areas of the lawn that require treatment.

Both power rakes and vertical cutters have depth settings; most have adjustable speed settings as well. Both tear out some grass plants along with the thatch. The vertical cutter is more effective on heavy thatch buildup, but may peel away turf when the machine is set for deep penetration and the grass has rooted into the thatch layer.

Use power rakes or vertical cutters when grass is actively growing—in the late spring or summer for warm-season grasses, in fall for cool-season grasses. (Dethatching cool-season grasses in spring causes too much damage to tender, newly emerging blades.) Make one pass, rake away the debris, make a second pass in the opposite direction, and rake again. Note that both power raking and vertical cutting create an enormous amount of debris. Before beginning, make arrangements for composting or disposal of the built-up material.

*Cores left on the surface help control thatch by topdressing the lawn.*

•To prevent thatch buildup and eliminate the damage done by mechanical dethatching, top-dress the soil annually with no more than ⅜ inch of organic matter, such as compost or topsoil. The microorganisms in the organic material will decompose the thatch layer gradually, over an extended period. However, if the thatch layer is ½ inch or thicker, power raking or vertical cutting will be needed.

## MOWING PROPERLY

Frequent, proper mowing helps grasses form a thick mass called turf or lawn. Grasses grow from the crown of the plant, rather than the tip. When some of the grass blade is mown off, the plant is stimulated to put out additional growth, lengthening the existing blades with more top growth, putting out new shoots from the crown, and developing new plants from stolons or rhizomes.

**Cut off the right amount of grass**  When the lawn is cut too short, the grasses must use energy and nutrients stored in their roots to replenish the top growth. No matter what type or types of grasses make up the lawn, cut off up to, but no more than, one third of the grass blade at each mowing. (See the chart at right for suggested grass lengths.)

**Change mowing direction**  Grass mowed in the same direction at every mowing is pressed down the same way and stressed in the same spots. Mow from the outside in, making a spiral pattern that goes clockwise one mowing, counterclockwise the next.

**Mow tall grass incrementally**  Rainy weather or a vacation can result in overgrown lawns. Use the adjustable blade-height setting to set the mower as high as possible, removing no more than one third of the length of the grass. After two or three days, lower the mower a notch and mow again. Follow this pattern for three or four mowings to bring the grass back to an acceptable height—and keep it healthy.

**Mow when the grass is dry**  Mowing wet grass can encourage the rapid spread of lawn diseases and put extra strain on the mower. To quick-dry the lawn, pull a rope, wire, or garden hose across the grass surface. Water will drop from the grass blades onto the soil. Wait 15 to

### Mowing Heights for Various Grasses

| Grass | Height |
|---|---|
| **Cool-Season Grasses** | |
| Annual ryegrass | 1½"–3½" |
| Bentgrass | ¼"–1" |
| Fine fescue | 1½"–3" |
| Kentucky bluegrass | 2"–4" |
| Perennial ryegrass | 1½"–3½" |
| Tall fescue | 2½"–4½" |
| **Warm-Season Grasses** | |
| Bahiagrass | 2"–4" |
| Bermudagrass (common) | ½"–1½" |
| Bermudagrass (improved) | ¼"–1" |
| Carpetgrass | 1"–2½" |
| Centipedegrass | 1"–2½" |
| St. Augustine grass | 2"–4" |
| Zoysiagrass | ½"–2" |
| **Native Grasses** | |
| Buffalograss | 1"–2½" |
| Wheatgrass | 2"–4" |

30 minutes, then check whether the grass is dry enough to mow. If it isn't, wait for safer conditions and follow the procedures for mowing tall grass.

**Leave the clippings**  When no more than one third of the grass blade is removed at a time, clippings may be safely left on the lawn. As they decompose, they will provide important nutrients to the soil, without contributing to thatch buildup.

## CONTROLLING PESTS AND DISEASES

The most effective control for pests and diseases is prevention. A healthy, vigorous lawn with a mix of grass types or cultivars is the best defense against problems.

**Follow correct cultural practices**  Lawns that are aerated and dethatched on a regular basis and mowed at the correct height will be thicker and healthier than neglected lawns and thus more resistant to pests. Adequate

*Leave the clippings on the lawn when mowing to preserve the nutrients in them. As they dry out, they will sift into the lawn and disappear.*

water and proper fertilization will also improve plant health and build resistance. As a first step in pest control, adjust your lawn maintenance techniques to provide the best possible growing conditions for the grass.

**Apply controls when the pests are active** Each insect goes through inactive stages in its life cycle, during which no controls will be effective. Learn a little about the attackers, and apply controls when they are actively feeding. Consult gardening books and qualified professionals for assistance.

**Identify the problem**   Sometimes it's hard to tell if a problem is caused by an insect, a disease, or a cultural difficulty, such as underwatering. Study the symptoms carefully, then consult *The Ortho Problem Solver* at your local garden center.

**Treat insect problems promptly**   Some insects can do serious damage to your lawn in a short time. Treat promptly and repeatedly until the problem is solved.

**Use fungicides to stop the spread of disease** Fungicides won't restore damaged grass, but they will help to keep the disease organisms from spreading into healthy grass. Lawn diseases usually occur during specific weather conditions. Some attack under snow; some during cool, wet weather; and some during the heat of summer. Protect the lawn with fungicides as long as conditions that favor the disease persist. When the weather changes, the lawn will repair the damage done by the disease with new growth.

**Plant a mix of grasses**   Each plant variety, and each cultivar within a variety, has a different level of resistance to certain disease organisms. One type of grass may be badly infected while other types remain strong. Plant a mix of varieties to keep disease from affecting the entire lawn.

## USING FERTILIZER

Fertilizers can stimulate turf growth, encourage one type of grass over another, force out weeds, and help the lawn cope with less than ideal conditions. Consult nursery professionals for help in choosing fertilizers that meet the needs of the grasses in the lawn and that work well for local growing conditions.

*The same broadcast spreader used to spread seed can spread fertilizer. Use this type of spreader for larger areas.*

**Apply fertilizer regularly**  For best growth, grasses need nitrogen, phosphorus, and potassium. Nitrogen encourages green, leafy growth. Phosphorus promotes root growth. Potassium increases general vigor and resistance to stress and diseases. Choose a complete fertilizer containing all three of these minerals. Plan a fertilizing program and follow it.

**Add fertilizer to warm-season grasses at regular intervals**  Warm-season grasses thrive in hot weather and become dormant in the winter if the temperature goes below freezing. They are mostly grown in the South. They need one feeding in early spring and a second in late spring, approximately one month later. Continue to fertilize at monthly intervals until growth slows in the fall.

**Feed cool-season grasses appropriately**  Cool-season grasses grow best in cool weather. They generally grow fast in the spring and fall, but slow down in the heat of summer. They do not become dormant in the winter. They are mostly used in the North. They do not need monthly applications of fertilizer. Give the heaviest feeding in the fall, as the weather cools; the next heaviest in early spring; and lighter feedings in late spring and late fall, after the grass stops growing. During the hot part of summer, feed only if the grass begins to turn light green, and then feed lightly.

**Check spreader output**  Mark off an area of 100 square feet (such as a square 10 feet by 10 feet) on a driveway or patio. Fill the hopper with fertilizer, adjust the setting, and run the spreader over the marked area. Sweep up the fertilizer and weigh it. This calibration shows you how much fertilizer the spreader is actually applying at the setting you select. If it's too much or too little (according to the quantities recommended on the fertilizer bag), try another setting. For the most even coverage, find a setting that puts on just half as much as recommended, then cover the lawn twice, in different directions.

The same method works with a handheld broadcast spreader, but the amount applied depends on the speed at which you walk as well as the spreader setting. Keep your speed constant for even coverage.

**Cover the perimeter first**  Apply fertilizer to the outer edges of the lawn first, by making a trip around the perimeter. As you cover the rest of the lawn, you can use the perimeter to turn the spreader around with the hopper closed.

**Apply weed-and-feed fertilizers when you expect weeds**  Use a combination fertilizer and preemergence herbicide in early spring, just before you expect weed seeds to germinate. In mild-winter areas, use it again in the fall, just before cool-season weeds germinate.

# WATERING

A healthy lawn can withstand short periods of inadequate moisture, but an extended water shortage depletes reserves and places the lawn under stress. To keep grass growing, provide supplemental water.

Without water, grasses revert to a semi-dormant or dormant state, nature's way of equalizing top growth with root growth. Drought-affected, brown lawns are unsightly, yet they will usually green up when moisture becomes available again. Check lawn books or ask garden-center personnel to recommend turf varieties and cultivars that best cope with prolonged dry conditions.

**Consider water supply**  Find out how much water your lawn actually needs. If water is rationed or scarce in your region, water only when the grass begins to wilt. If you have adequate water, apply enough to replace the soil moisture used by the grass.

**Look for footprints**  Drought-stressed grass lacks the resiliency of normal lawns. Walk across an open area, then turn and examine the turf. If your footprints are visible, the grass is wilting and needs water.

**Note wilting**  Watch turf areas for signs of lack of water. A leaf blade wilts by rolling or folding on its long axis. This exposes the bottom of the blade and gives the wilted section a dull or dark cast. The appearance of dull spots in the lawn is the sign that the grass needs watering soon.

**Check for soil moisture**  With a hand-aerator or trowel, dig out a 12-inch-long core of grass and soil. Healthy grass roots should go 12 inches deep. The drier the soil at that depth, the more critical the water need.

**See if you watered deeply enough**  If the soil has become very dry, it is hard to the touch and resists penetration by a sharp object, such as a screwdriver. After watering, poke a long-shanked screwdriver into the soil. It will penetrate the newly moistened soil easily, but stop at the dry soil. You can use this method to be sure you are applying water evenly (by poking different spots) or to see if you watered long enough. If the wet soil is only a few inches

deep, leave the sprinklers on longer. Each watering should wet the soil at least 1 foot deep.

**Water only when necessary**  During periods of active growth, most turfgrasses need 1 inch of water per week (or up to 2 inches in very hot, dry, windy weather)—water that penetrates a foot or so into the soil. Measure rainfall with a rain gauge. If nature doesn't supply at least an inch each week, the lawn needs extra watering. On the other hand, if rainfall adds up to an inch a week and the rain seems to be penetrating the soil adequately, there is no need to water.

**Water thoroughly to encourage deep rooting**  Soak the lawn, then let it dry before watering it again. Frequent, light sprinklings encourage grass roots to stay close to the soil surface, where they are susceptible to heat and drying. In dry summer weather, water most lawn varieties every third day. Be sure each irrigation is deep enough to replenish the water lost since the last watering.

**Measure water applications**  Place sprinklers in the usual positions on the lawn, set to produce the spray patterns you normally use. Place several containers with straight sides (most tin

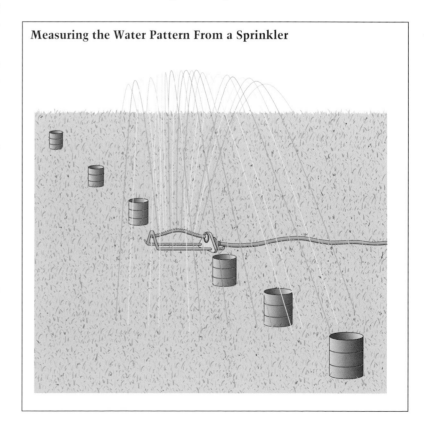

**Measuring the Water Pattern From a Sprinkler**

*Water early in the morning to save water and to let the grass dry before people walk on it.*

cans work well) at various places in the typical spray pattern: at the outer edges, toward the middle, and close to the sprinkler. Let the sprinkler run at normal pressure for a set period of time. Measure the amount of water in each of the cans. Determine the rate at which the sprinklers are applying water and check for an even pattern of spray distribution. Dig out a core of soil to check how deeply the water has penetrated. This method measures both the amount of water you apply and the evenness of the distribution. From it you may learn that you need to adjust the pattern, change the pressure, or alter the watering time.

Make the necessary adjustments when the lawn next needs water. Set out the cans and time the sprinklers again. After the sprinklers have run for the newly designated period, measure the water in the cans, and check the soil.

It may take one or two more measuring sessions to establish how long the sprinklers need to be run to supply sufficient water. Once the time is set, let the sprinklers run for that period each time to ensure deep watering.

**Water early in the day**   There are many good reasons to use sprinklers in the early morning: commercial demands are fewer, so the water pressure is greater; there is little or no wind; the irrigation won't interfere with other activities; and the grass will dry more quickly.

Watering during the heat of the day will not damage plants, but more of the water (as much as 10 percent in hot, dry weather) will be lost to evaporation.

**Let the grass grow taller in a drought**   During water shortages mow less often and raise the mower height to keep the grass a little longer. As usual, remove no more than one third of the grass blade in any one mowing. Taller grass shades the surrounding plants and the soil, cutting moisture evaporation. Less frequent mowing allows the blade tips to use food stored in the blades, without drawing as many nutrients from the roots.

**Reduce fertilizer use during drought**   Feed drought-affected grass sparingly until normal rainfall resumes. Slow-release organic fertilizers, which increase the level of soil microorganisms and organic matter, may be beneficial.

**Cool the grass in hot weather**   Cool-weather grasses suffer during extremely hot weather. The added stress makes them more susceptible to diseases, and their growth slows. During very hot periods, wet the lawn in the early afternoon. Apply only enough water to wet the grass blades and the very surface of the soil; this water will evaporate in the next hour or so, cooling the grass and relieving stress.

# FIXING PROBLEM AREAS

The low spots, high spots, and bare spots in your lawn can be repaired.

**Top-dress low spots**   Raise low spots in the lawn by applying a topdressing of fine soil ½ inch deep. Spread it evenly over the surface of the lawn. Use a leaf rake to gently brush the soil off the grass blades. Wait two to three weeks and repeat. Continue this process until the soil has reached the desired level. Don't rush. Too much soil applied at one time will smother the turf.

**Shave high spots**   Carefully remove the existing turf over the high spot. With a sharp spade, cut the area into strips as wide as the spade and about 6 feet long. Cut the turf from one strip at a time by slicing with the spade just under the matted layer of stems on the surface, to loosen a layer about ¾ inch thick. Roll up the strip as you go.

Eliminate the high spot by removing as much soil as necessary. Be sure to replace the layer of topsoil. Rake and smooth the area so that it will be level with the existing grade when the turf sections are reset. Replace the turf sections in the same manner as you would lay sod.

**Aerate compacted areas**   On heavily used areas of turf, use a core-type aerator to loosen the soil and restore the free flow of oxygen and water to the grass roots. (See page 46 for tips on aerating.)

**Create a proper path**   A shortcut carved through the lawn is often best converted to a proper pathway. Replace turf with a path of pebbles, shredded bark, or stepping-stones and ground cover.

**Treat "dog spots"**   Lawn spots made by dogs usually turn dark green, then dull gray or blue-green, before browning. If you see the dog urinate, wash the spot with water immediately to dilute the salts and wash them beyond the root zone. If the lawn is not well fertilized, the nitrogen in the urine will cause a bright green ring around the dead spot. To make these spots less noticeable, keep the lawn bright green by adding fertilizer regularly. Fertilizer spills can be treated the same way as urine spots. Pick up

---

## Glossary of Lawn Terms

**Cultivar**   Short for cultivated variety. Refers to plants selected for certain characteristics and then propagated to reproduce those characteristics.

**Dormant**   The latent, or inactive, stage when plant top growth is suspended until more favorable conditions exist.

**Mulch**   Material used to cover the soil surface to provide plant protection or aesthetic appeal.

**Plug**   A small piece of sod complete with soil, roots, and blades.

**Rhizome**   An underground stem that grows horizontally under the soil surface. New plants can form at the joints.

**Sprig**   Small sections of stolons or rhizomes, each with nodes or joints from which roots can emerge and form new plants. A sprig usually has small tufts of grass blades at its top and, sometimes, other tufts scattered along its length. Sprigs are sold individually by the bushel, or as sections of sod that are gently pulled apart to yield sprigs.

**Stolon**   An aboveground stem that grows along the soil surface and is capable of forming new plants. At each joint, or node, roots can develop and send up new plants.

**Thatch**   The matted layer of grass stolons, rhizomes, and plant debris that gathers at the soil surface, restricting the flow of water, nutrients, and air into the soil and to grass roots.

---

all the fertilizer you can, then flush the spot well with water.

**Patch dead spots**   Dead spots caused by dog urine, gasoline or fertilizer spills, or disease can be patched with healthy sod. First fix the problem that caused the dead spot. Urine and fertilizer are water soluble and can be flushed out of the soil with a few waterings. Gasoline, oil, or other insoluble chemicals can be washed out with dishwater. Flush the soil several times with old dishwater (or make dishwater with a couple of tablespoons of dish soap in a gallon of water), then flush it several times with clean water to remove the soap.

Cut a patch of sod from the edge of the lawn or an inconspicuous spot. Lay the patch over the dead spot and use a spade to cut it to fit. Remove the patch, then use the spade to cut the dead spot from the lawn. Insert the patch.

**Keep a sod nursery**   If you have frequent need for patching material, designate a section of ground in an inconspicuous place as a sod nursery. As you remove patches, replace them with a few plugs cut from another section of the nursery. The plugs will grow to fill in the missing sod. Plugs can easily be cut with a bulb planter.

# Providing Plant Care

*Landscapes display a panorama of plants—from arching trees and evergreen and deciduous shrubs to perennial and annual flowers, ground covers, and grasses. Each plant, itself an object of beauty, should complement surrounding plantings.*

The middle range of the landscape—above the turf and beneath the trees—displays the most versatility and freedom of style. The types of plants chosen for this range, the manner in which they are placed, the method of pruning and general care, the frequency of new plantings, all reflect the preferences of the gardener. And many home gardeners look to nursery professionals for guidance in providing care for this range of plants.

Because they deal with a large variety of plants, nursery professionals tend to be generalists. These pros include field and container growers, greenhouse growers, nursery and garden-center managers, conservatory and arboretum horticulturists, park and public-land managers, landscape contractors, and design or building specialists. Nursery pros strive to grow healthy, well-formed plants, studying and adapting techniques to achieve the best results with the most efficient methods. The pros learn the growing habits of plants, the quirks of the environment, the successful cultural techniques, and the way to maintain a beneficial balance between harmful and helpful organisms.

The love of plants is often the driving force behind a person's choice to enter the nursery business. Nursery professionals invest much time and effort in producing and maintaining plants. Their commitment extends to giving advice on proper plant care in home landscapes so the plants continue to thrive and so others can gain the greatest enjoyment from them. The tips from the nursery pros will help you grow vigorous plants with a minimal output of time and energy.

*The right plant care pays off in gardens like this one.*

## SELECTING AND PLANTING NURSERY PLANTS

Planting methods vary according to the type of plant, its stage of growth, and the planting site and conditions. Sometimes long-established methods are still the most effective; in other instances, new technology and research have improved time-honored techniques.

**Choose healthy plants**  Examine plants closely for signs of damage or stress. One broken branch may be overlooked, but several damaged branches, scuffed bark, and dry or water-soaked roots signal poor shipping and handling care—and future problems.

•Bare-root plants should be dormant, with moist packing material or shredded bark around the roots, or a similar method of keeping the plant from drying out. Look for pliable branches, swollen buds, green color beneath the bark, and full root systems with a well-formed network of large and small roots. Avoid plants with dry buds; dying twigs and branch tips; fully developed foliage; discoloration; or damaged, withered, or poorly formed roots.

•Container plants may be dormant or actively growing, depending on the time of year. Select plants with a relatively symmetrical formation of branches, healthy foliage color and growth, and healthy root development in balance with the size of the top growth. If top growth is sturdy, with spreading branches, root growth should be extensive. Small feeder roots should be visible at the outer edges of the soil ball. Large, chopped-off roots may indicate that the specimen is a recently potted bare-root plant. A trunk or stem that seems too thick for the size of the container indicates that the plant has remained in the same container too long and may have difficulty adjusting to being planted in the garden. Avoid container plants with broken branches, insect- or disease-damaged foliage, multiple pruning cuts that are just beginning to seal over, or soil that has pulled away from the sides of the container.

•Check for girdling roots on trees. If a root is wrapped tightly around the trunk, it will slowly choke the tree as the trunk expands. Check just below the surface of the soil to see if a root is tightly encircling the trunk. Girdling roots on shrubs or other plants do no damage.

•Balled-and-burlapped plants should exhibit the same general characteristics as container plants. Check the wrapped rootball. It should be firm and evenly moist. Avoid balled-and-burlapped plants with dry, crumbling rootballs and those whose soil has pulled away from the main plant stem. Also avoid any plant that can be moved easily within the soil mass.

**Have the nursery hold the plant until you are ready**  Most nurseries will hold purchased plants for a few days or weeks, until you are ready to plant. This is especially handy if you are planning a large job, such as landscaping a yard. You can make your selections at your leisure, then have your purchases delivered the day before you wish to plant.

**Protect plants on the trip home**  Always lift plants from the bottom, never by the main stem or branches. Be careful not to loosen or jar the soil of container plants and balled-and-burlapped plants. If the plants are in the back

*Select container plants with healthy foliage and good root development. Slip the plant from the container to check the root system.*

of a pickup or otherwise exposed, drive slowly and cover any exposed foliage with plastic or burlap to avoid wind damage and desiccation.

**Prepare the plants** If planting a bare-root plant, trim off any damaged roots. If few tiny feeder roots are visible, snip an inch or two from each root. Before planting, soak the root systems in a pail of water for several, but not more than 24, hours. Before planting container plants or balled-and-burlapped plants, water them so the soil surrounding their roots will be moist but not soggy. Moist soil adheres to roots when you remove the container or wrap; dry soil falls away.

**Dig a planting hole that works** Use a sharp spade or shovel to mark the circumference of the hole. Plan to dig a hole two to three times wider than the root mass, and follow the steps in the next list.

•Work inward from the outside of the circle. If you need sod for patching turf, skim off sod and place it to one side on a piece of tarp. If not, add the sod to the compost pile. Remove the layer of topsoil, shoveling it onto the tarp into a stack. Dig out the remainder of the soil, placing it in a separate pile. Make the hole deep enough to set the plant at, or slightly above, its depth in the nursery soil. (A color

change on the bark indicates this level. Bark that was below the soil is significantly darker or lighter than bark exposed to sunlight.)

•Use a sharp spade or cultivator to rough up the sides of the hole. This will help lessen the texture difference between backfill soil and native soil and encourage tender roots to stretch beyond the backfill.

*Top: Soak the roots of bare-root plants for several hours before planting. Bottom: A tarp makes cleanup easy after digging the planting hole.*

**Bareroot Planting**

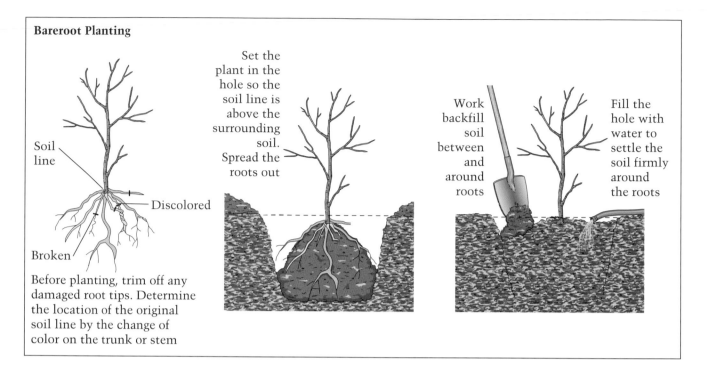

Soil line

Discolored

Broken

Before planting, trim off any damaged root tips. Determine the location of the original soil line by the change of color on the trunk or stem

Set the plant in the hole so the soil line is above the surrounding soil. Spread the roots out

Work backfill soil between and around roots

Fill the hole with water to settle the soil firmly around the roots

• If the soil is heavy and packed, use a spade to rough up the soil at the base of the planting hole. Make allowance for this loose soil when positioning the plant. After repeated waterings the plant will gradually sink to the level of the solid soil base.

**Prepare the backfill soil**   If the native soil is heavy clay or light sand, mix organic matter (such as compost) with the soil from the hole. Use up to one third organic matter, by mass. If the native soil is rich, well-drained loam, no soil amendments are necessary.

**Use a shovel to check plant position**   Gently lower the plant into the hole (leaving the container or burlap in place) to check for proper hole depth. In heavy clay soil, place the plant a few inches above the surrounding soil to maintain adequate drainage. In rich loam or sandy soil, position the plant so that the top of the rootball is level with the soil surface. Lay a shovel handle across the hole to check the positioning. Remove the plant and adjust the soil level as needed.

**Create a raised planting mound**   In heavy clay soil, position the plant a little high and mound soil around the trunk or stem to the level at which the plant was set in the nursery soil. (Look for color change on bark.) Extend this soil mound approximately 2 feet away from

the trunk or stem in all directions. This modified raised bed will keep excess water from accumulating around the base of the plant.

**Use puddling to plant a bare-root plant**   With the roots spread around the mound at the bottom of the hole and the plant at the proper level, begin adding the backfill. When the hole is half filled, fill the hole with water and allow it to soak in. Fill the hole with backfill, and water again. The puddling process eliminates air pockets.

**Score the rootball when planting a container plant**   Remove the plant from a plastic or metal can. Use a cultivator or knife to score the sides and bottom of the rootball. These cuts stimulate the plant roots to send out new growth. Replace the plant in the hole. Fiber or peat pots may be left on the plant, but strip away any rim that extends above the rootball and slash the bottom and sides in several places. Fill the hole as you would for a bare-root plant.

**Remove wrap last when planting a balled-and-burlapped plant**   With the plant positioned in the hole, cut and remove the cord around the top of the rootball and any cord around the trunk or branches. If the wrap is natural burlap, it will slowly disintegrate; you may roll it back and tuck it around the base of

## Planting From Containers

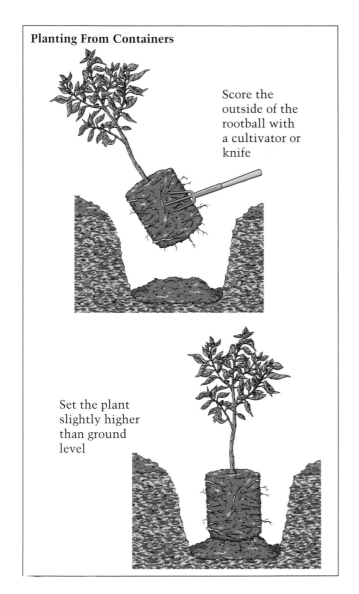

Score the outside of the rootball with a cultivator or knife

Set the plant slightly higher than ground level

## Planting Balled-and-Burlapped Plants

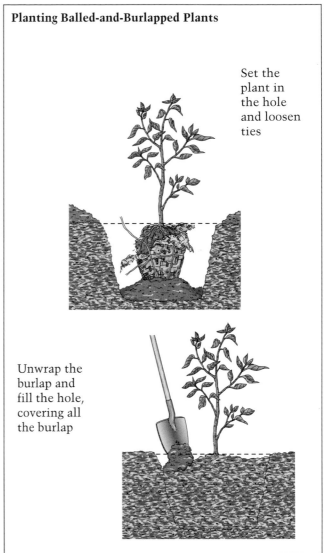

Set the plant in the hole and loosen ties

Unwrap the burlap and fill the hole, covering all the burlap

the rootball. (Be sure all burlap edges are buried.) Synthetic material should be removed.

**Leave the can on when positioning large plants** Trees or shrubs in 15-gallon cans are heavy and difficult to move. These cans usually have a wire handle on each side of the rim. The handles can make the heavy plant easier to position in the hole, and the container can protect the rootball from breaking. Remove the bottom of the can with a hatchet, and then position the plant in the hole. It may be necessary to lift the plant out and adjust the depth of the hole. When the hole is the right depth and the plant is in it, cut down the side of the can and unwrap it from the rootball.

**Form a water retention basin** For plants placed at soil level in well-drained loam or sandy soil, form a ridge of soil 3 to 4 inches

high all the way around the planting hole. Make the ridge higher if there's a mulch layer, to keep the top of the ridge above the level of the mulch.

Water the new plant by filling the basin you have created between the plant and the ridge. The ridge will ensure that the water sinks into the root zone. Use the basin to water until the plant is well established—a few weeks in warm weather. During wet weather, remove a portion of the ridge to allow excess rainwater to drain away.

**Add mulch** Newly planted trees and shrubs should be protected against harsh and drying weather conditions with a 3- to 4-inch layer of mulch over the soil surface. The mulch will also help to control weeds. Keep the material 6 to 8 inches back from the trunk or crown of the plant to avoid crown rot.

**Water ex-container plants frequently in hot weather**   Until the roots begin growing into the soil around them, plants recently out of containers need watering as often as they did in their containers. Fill the water retention basin frequently—perhaps daily—during hot, dry weather.

**Prune bare-root deciduous shrubs severely**
Wait to prune bare-root trees until after they have leafed out. Leave branches 3 to 6 inches long. Then trim off any dead branches, leaving all the healthy branches at full length. The healthy branches will help feed the plant during the critical first season. Remove growth along the lower trunk only when it reaches pencil thickness.

**Plant roses to preserve the variety**   Hybrid roses are grafted to the rootstock of sturdier varieties so the hybrids gain vigor, hardiness, and strength.

•In cold regions, place the bud union approximately 1 inch below ground level, so the rose will be protected even when harsh winter freezes cause it to die back to the ground. If planted too deep, however, the rose may not bloom or it could develop crown rot.

•In warm climates, place the bud union at ground level so the rose does not send out roots above the graft. Roots from above the graft

## Perennials With Special Needs

**Bougainvillea**   Plant potted bougainvillea carefully, without disturbing the rootball. Its roots are brittle and slow to send out new growth. Plant in sunny, sheltered locations.

**Clematis**   Plant young clematis so that the lowest pair of buds is below the soil surface. Deep planting will preserve the plants if harsh winters kill the tops back to ground level. Clematis plants need alkaline soil and must have cool roots to bloom. Mulch heavily or plant a ground cover around the plant to keep the soil cool.

**Daylilies**   Plant daylilies in September to bloom the next season. Bare-root daylilies and daylilies in small containers will not have enough vigor to bloom the same year if they are planted in spring.

**Peonies**   Bush-type peonies need to be positioned carefully, with the bud below the soil surface but less than 2 inches below (1 inch or less in heavy clay soils). Planted incorrectly, they will not bloom. Tree peonies may be planted with the union as deep as 6 inches below ground level.

**Wildflowers**   Wildflowers will naturalize, but they need pampering during their first year. Good drainage is essential. Weeds need to be kept out; the tender young plants cannot compete. Heavy mulch may result in crown rot.

*Select perennials from the many varieties available from local nurseries and garden centers.*

**Planting Bulbs**

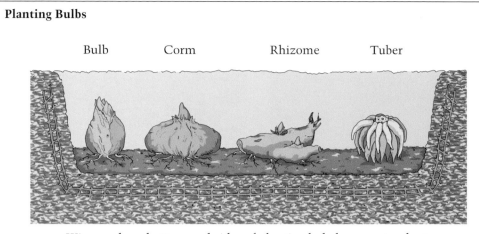

Bulb        Corm        Rhizome        Tuber

Wire mesh on bottom and sides of planting hole keeps out rodents

would be those of the weaker hybrid rose, less able to support vigorous growth. If the graft is above ground level, the rootstock may send out shoots of its own. Top growth from the rootstock would be that of the hardier plant, usually a rugged, but not particularly attractive, rose.

**Plant containers anytime**   Plant container perennials any time you can work the soil. To remove plants from the container, spread fingers around the plant and over the soil. Turn the container over. Tap the rim lightly while keeping the container upside down to dislodge the plant.

Score the sides and bottom of the soil mass to stimulate root development. Position the plant with its most attractive side outward, considering also the effects of prevailing winds, the seasonal sun and shade patterns, and the impact the transplant will have on surrounding plants. Set the plant at the same level relative to the soil surface as it was in the container.

**Plant bare-root perennials early**   Most bare-root perennials are available in early spring. Planted early they establish an extensive root system before temperatures drop. Spread the roots gently when setting the plants. Pinch back the top growth to one half. Fill in soil, watering to remove air pockets.

**Control invasive varieties**   Plant rapidly spreading perennial varieties inside a container to keep them from overrunning beds. To do this, cut the bottom from a 5-gallon plastic container and sink it into the soil. Position it so about 1 inch of the container is above the surface.

**Make a wall around bamboo**   Running bamboo—but not the clumping types—can be one of the most invasive plants in the garden. If possible, plant it where its roots will be restricted by paths, driveways, or house foundations. If this isn't possible, dig a trench about a foot deep around the bamboo bed and fill it with concrete to keep the bamboo in its place. Watch to be sure the bamboo doesn't send runners over the top of this underground wall.

**Plant bulbs for guaranteed flowering**   Although a small crocus corm looks quite different from a begonia tuber, both are often treated like true bulbs and planted in a similar fashion. Bulbs are a specialized group of perennial plants that retain a reserve of nutrients in an underground storage base. Because the flower is already developed within the bulb and all its food is stored around it, bulbs will bloom under almost any conditions and require very little maintenance after planting.

**Store bulbs at cool temperatures**   Provide air circulation and some protection—such as sand, vermiculite, or shredded paper—to keep bulbs from becoming wet or drying out during storage. Some bulbs that dry out quickly, such as lilies, are normally stored in moist, shredded wood and packed in plastic bags. Plant lilies as soon as possible after purchase.

**Plant bulbs at the right time**   Bulbs that bloom in spring are planted in the fall; those that bloom in summer and fall, in the spring. In warm western and southern regions some spring-flowering bulbs need a cooling period to

*Left: Plant bulbs in large groups for striking displays. Shown here are gladiolus bulbs. Right: These flowering and near-flowering annuals provide color as soon as you plant them. Those that aren't actually blooming yet will bloom within a couple of weeks of planting, and generally transplant more satisfactorily.*

bloom. Obtain precooled bulbs or allow adequate time to refrigerate them before planting, usually six to eight weeks.

**Pick healthy bulbs**   Generally, the bigger the bulb, the better the flower. Look for firm bulbs with no soft or discolored spots. A loose or partially removed papery cover on true bulbs or bulblets is not necessarily an indication of damage. Double and triple bulbs (bulbs with offsets) are a bargain. The larger bulb will flower the first season; the smaller side bulbs will develop in another year or two. A light pinkish area around the buds, sometimes seen on gladiolus bulbs or begonia tubers, indicates early development and good health.

**Pick an appropriate planting depth**   As a general rule, plant at two to three times the depth of the bulb. Plant deeper in warm regions to allow the bulb to chill completely. Deep planting keeps a bulb from multiplying as rapidly as it would in a shallow hole. Plant shallow to encourage spreading and naturalization; plant deep to protect from gophers.

**Use mesh to keep animals away from bulbs**   If burrowing animals are a problem, line the planting hole with wire mesh. Chicken wire

with a 1-inch mesh will keep out pocket gophers. Use welded wire fabric with $\frac{1}{2}$-inch mesh to exclude meadow mice.

**Plant bulbs in groups**   Because bulbs make the most striking show when they are planted in groups, dig a trench or large bed rather than individual holes. Position the bulbs in the hole and fill it in.

**Create a surprise by planting bulbs in flower beds and ground covers**   Use a bulb planter to plant individual bulbs in beds devoted to other kinds of plants, such as ground covers or perennials. Most bulbs emerge and bloom early in the spring, and garden visitors are surprised to find flowers in unexpected places. As the bulb foliage turns yellow in late spring or summer, the ground cover or perennials grow up to hide it.

**Plant tulips flat side out**   When planting a group of tulips in a pot for forcing or bringing indoors in the spring, position them with the flat side toward the outside. The first leaves will curl toward the flat side, making a more attractive pot.

**Plant annuals for quick color**   Started plants—the small, potted ones often sold by nurseries and garden centers as bedding plants—have spent weeks developing in a greenhouse. They provide gardeners a chance to get a head start in creating flower displays. Plant started plants in large beds as early as possible. In mild-climate areas, make two plantings a year: one in mid-April and the other, of cool-weather flowers, in early October.

**Choose small plants**   Look for dark, healthy foliage; closely spaced and symmetrical branching; and sturdy stems. Choose smaller plants that have not flowered yet. Small plants transplant with less shock and usually do not need to be pinched back at the time of planting. Larger plants, already blooming, are more attractive in the nursery, but cost more and don't re-establish themselves as easily as smaller plants.

**Shade transplants**   In hot weather, cover transplants with a lath screen, a slatted box, or a handful of straw; or stick a shingle into the ground on the sunny side of the plants. Shade them in this fashion until they are well established—usually a few days to a week. Keep them well watered during this period.

## USING SMALL PLANTS IN THE LANDSCAPE

Some of the most dramatic landscaping effects are created in the middle range, between the turf and the trees. Evergreen and deciduous shrubs provide backdrops, screen and soften sharp foundation angles, and hide unsightly views. Ground covers hold hillsides and fill in corners. Magnificent blossoms unfold from shrubs, such as lilacs, roses, rhododendrons, and azaleas.

The large, woody plants are usually a critical part of the landscape design. Often, the perennials, bulbs, ornamental grasses, and annuals are added later, when the main landscaping has been completed.

**Mix beds of perennials and bulbs**   For a long-lasting flower display, plant spring-flowering bulbs among summer-flowering perennials. The fading foliage of spring-flowering plants will be masked by the emerging blossoms of the summer flowers. Slip spring-flowering bulbs into the soil around perennials. Place the point of the trowel or the circle of the bulb

planter just beyond the foliage tips. Disturb as little soil as possible, making a hole just large enough to set the bulb in place. Firm the soil; water well.

**Plant perennials and annuals next to bulbs**   Dig individual planting holes for perennials and annuals next to the foliage of flowering bulbs. As the foliage of the bulbs dies back, the annuals and perennials will flourish.

**Plant perennials over a bulb bed**   In fall, plant perennials in the top layers of soil over bulb beds. The bulbs will come through in the spring, without damaging the perennials.

*Top: Annuals provide an explosion of spring color to this mixed border. Bottom: Bulbs fill in with color while the perennials are still developing in a perennial border. This waterlily tulip (Tulipa kaufmanniana 'Heart's Desire') naturalizes and persists for many years in the garden, unlike most other tulips, which are short-lived.*

**Plant annuals alone**   If you will be changing the annuals in a bed once or twice a year, don't plant anything else in the bed with them. If the annuals are alone, it's easy to pull them all out, till the bed, and plant fresh flowers. If bulbs, perennials, or shrubs share the bed, they interfere with the tilling.

**Root-prune plants to control their size**
When a container plant reaches its optimum size for the site, or a particularly choice container, use a sharply pointed trowel, or long, sharp knife, to prune the roots. Place the trowel near the container edge, approximately two thirds of the distance from the central stem of the plant to the edge of the container. Slowly sink the trowel into the soil. Stop pushing if the trowel meets heavy resistance; major roots should not be severed. When the trowel meets only limited resistance, push it all the way to the bottom of the container. Then pull the trowel straight up and move it over slightly, then sink it again. Make four to six insertions, spacing them evenly around the plant. Repeat this process at different places in the container every four to eight weeks as necessary to keep growth controlled.

## PROPAGATING PLANTS

Many plants are easy to multiply—you just follow a few simple steps. Other plants require a precise combination of temperature, humidity, nutrients, and light-and-dark cycles for success. These plants are best grown under specialized greenhouse conditions.

**Consider growing your own plants from seed**
There are three reasons to grow plants from seed. The first: Many more species and varieties are available from seed catalogs than from plant nurseries. The second: Seeds are much less expensive than grown plants. The third: the satisfaction you get from watching the miracle of germination and growth.

**Sterilize pots, flats, and equipment**   Give seeds the best chance of survival by providing a sterile environment. In soap and warm water, wash seed trays, pots, and any tools you'll use; clean away dirt and residue. Rinse the equipment in a solution of 1 cup liquid bleach to 4 gallons water, and allow them to air-dry.

## Encouraging Germination

Many seeds will germinate in a week or two without special treatment. Some, however, can take as long as two years to germinate. Here are some tips to speed the germination of slow starters.

**Soak**   Some seeds have a hard natural coating that needs to soften for germination. Soak these seeds for a day in water.

**Scarify**   Seeds with especially hard seed coats will germinate only if there's an opening in the seed coat. Scarify (make a small opening in) these seeds by nicking them with a nail file, knife, or sandpaper.

**Cool**   Some seeds need a period of chilling to break dormancy and germinate. Place these seeds in a sealed plastic bag with damp peat moss or vermiculite, and store them in the refrigerator for the winter; plant in the spring.

**Protect**   Some seeds are very sensitive to heat and humidity and come in a special foil-coated package within the regular seed packet. Once this pack is opened, plant the seed at once or its ability to germinate will drop drastically.

**Provide light**   Certain seeds need light for germination, so they must be covered with only a very fine layer of soil or none at all. For these seeds follow instructions precisely; just a small amount of extra soil over the seed will reduce the percentage of seeds that germinate and may prevent any from germinating.

**Use a sterile seed-starting mix**   Buy a prepared seed mix, or make one using sphagnum moss, vermiculite, and perlite. Regular garden soil can be sterilized but is generally too heavy to allow seed germination. Before sowing, wet the mix well. Be especially thorough in wetting a dry soilless mix, which will tend to shed rather than absorb water.

**Start seeds late rather than early**   Check seed package labels or seed catalogs for the length of the germination period, the number of days to maturity, and the suggested planting date. Count the days backward from the suggested planting date to find out when to start the plants. It is better to sow late and set out small plants than to sow early and have to hold back overgrown seedlings until the weather permits planting.

**Use peat moss to avoid damping off** Small seedlings are susceptible to a fungal disease called damping off. The fungus attacks the seedling at the soil line, making it fall over and killing it. Peat moss impedes the growth of this fungus. Sow seeds on the surface of sterile potting soil, then sift peat moss over them, about ¼ inch deep. Place a pane of glass across the container or stretch plastic across it; this will help keep the soil moist. If condensation forms on the glass or plastic, vent it a bit to allow air circulation.

**Provide bright light** Use a sunny south window or fluorescent plant lights to provide bright light. Place plant lights a few inches above the soil. As the seedlings grow, raise the lights to maintain the same distance to the lights. The warmer the temperature, the more important it is to have bright light. If you can't provide a spot bright enough, put the seedlings in a cool (50° to 65°F) room.

**Maintain adequate humidity** To keep humidity levels high, stretch a sheet of plastic or burlap across the top of the container. Or place a section of glass just above the soil surface, supporting it on the sides of the container. Maintaining adequate humidity is especially necessary if you start seeds indoors during late winter, when heating dries the indoor air.

Remove the coverings to water the seeds, then replace them. When the seedlings grow to reach the covering, remove it and mist the seedlings to supplement the humidity level.

**Harden off the plants** Before moving plants outside, greenhouse growers harden them off by reducing the heat and increasing the ventilation. Although it's often not possible to reduce the heat indoors without disturbing family comfort, you can acclimate the plants to the outdoors by reducing watering and taking them outdoors for short periods.

• Two weeks before the desired planting date, begin to cut back on watering. Allow plants to dry slightly, but water them before the wilting stage.

• Set plants outdoors in a shaded spot, sheltered from strong winds. Start with an hour or two of exposure, gradually building up to full days. Bring them back indoors overnight to avoid frost damage.

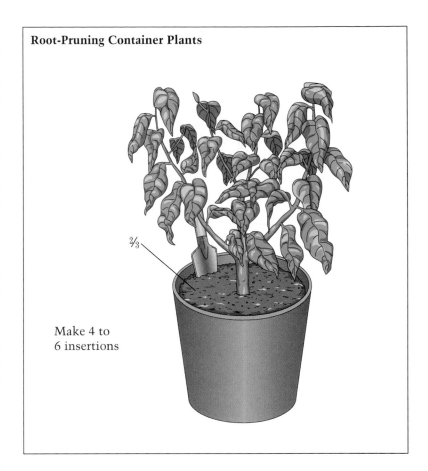

**Root-Pruning Container Plants**

⅔

Make 4 to 6 insertions

**Sow seeds outdoors for easy starting** If plants need special treatment to germinate or if you want seedlings to set out as early as possible, start the plants in containers indoors. But if you don't care about early plants and the seeds will grow naturally in your area, plant them directly in the ground and let nature do the work.

**Mix small seed with sand for even distribution** Seeds that are so tiny they are difficult to pick up individually are easier to sow in rows or over a fixed area when mixed with sand. Determine how much sand will cover the sowing area by spreading some without the seed. A measuring cup or a small paper cup squeezed to form a pouring spout will help guide the sand to the right spot. Gently mix together the predetermined amount of sand and the correct amount of seed for the area. From the cup, pour the mixture evenly over the area.

**Germinate seeds in gel** Seeds can be germinated in moistened gel, put into plastic bags, and the sprouted seedlings squeezed out into a furrow. This method results in fast starting. It is a good way to plant very small seeds, or to start seeds during weather that is too hot or too cold for germinating seeds.

Germinate the seeds by sprinkling them on a damp paper towel and rolling it loosely, then inserting it in a plastic bag. Place the towel in a warm place, such as on the top of a refrigerator until the seeds just begin to germinate.

Make a gel by adding a small amount of cornstarch to water (about a tablespoon to a quart) and heating it until the cornstarch thickens. Cool the gel and thin it to the consistency of raw egg white.

Gently mix the germinating seeds into the gel, put the gel into a plastic bag and close the top. Move to the furrow and cut off one corner of the bag. Squeeze the gel and seeds through this hole into the planting furrow; cover the seeds with soil as usual. The seeds will be evenly spaced, and will emerge within a couple of days. This trick works well with carrots and other small seeds.

**Press furrows for even moisture**   After preparing the soil in a seedbed, make furrows for small seeds by pressing the soil with the edge of a board. Press quite firmly, so the soil under the board is compressed. This compression allows moisture to move upward by capillary action, to replace moisture lost during the day.

**Cover seeds with sand**   Cover small seeds in furrows with white sand. The sand is easy to see against dark soil, so there is no need to

mark the rows. Also, the sand will not crust or impede the growth of the germinating plant. Because sand dries out more quickly than soil, make the covering a little deeper than if you were covering rows with soil.

**Start plants by division**   Many annuals and herbaceous perennials can be multiplied by simple division—plants are dug from the soil (roots and all), cut apart, and the now-separate pieces replanted. Professional gardeners use this method to rejuvenate old planting beds and start new ones.

**Dig up a large clump**   Start digging at the outer fringe of leaves to avoid cutting the main roots. Use a spade or shovel to slice a ring around the plant, moving deep into the soil until only a few tiny roots are visible. Slice across the bottom of the soil ball, then use the spade to lift the entire plant from the hole.

Rinse the soil away from the roots by gently swirling them in a bucket of water. Once the roots are exposed, it's easier to divide the plant. (Spray from a hose may damage the tender feeder roots and slow plant growth.)

**Cut or pull apart natural groupings**   Follow the natural pattern made by the stem groupings to determine where to make the divisions. Look for several stems originating from one area, or a new plant that has emerged from the roots. Generally, separation is relatively easy.

**Starting Plants by Division**

Dig clump, starting at outer fringe of leaves. Dig down, around, and across bottom.

Slip fingers between 2 stem groupings and separate. Use pitchforks to separate large clumps.

Slip fingers between two stem groupings and pull them apart gently. When the roots are heavy, tough, and entwined, cut the plant apart with a sharp knife; or, drive two garden forks into the clump, back to back, and pull on the forks in opposite directions to pry apart the entangled roots. If you use a knife, disinfect it in rubbing alcohol, or a bleach and water solution, between each cut.

Separate vigorous growth from the old core, or center of the plant, which frequently becomes woody and unproductive as plants mature. Discard any parts that are soft, especially woody, or showing signs of decline.

Trim the top growth back to about 2½ inches so the roots won't have so much foliage to support as they recover from division. Dig the planting holes deep enough to set the divisions at the same depth as the parent plant. Spread the roots, gently filling in soil around them. Puddle-in the backfill.

Some perennials have specific needs.

•Divide peonies so that there are three to five buds, or eyes, on each division.

•Cut tuberous begonias into sections with one bud each.

•Divide lily bulbs by removing the outer scales; taking one or two layers from each bulb will not damage the parent.

•Divide iris rhizomes into sections with one shoot each.

**Make divisions without uprooting the original plant**   Use a sharp spade to cut one or two wedges from the crown of the actively growing parent plant. Cut straight down on all three sides to cleanly sever the roots. Lift out the divisions from the outer edge and plant them. Fill in the empty spaces around the parent plant with rich humus or compost, tamping it down to eliminate air pockets.

**Start plants by layering**   Layering is the easiest and surest way to propagate plants, but it can also be one of the slowest. Vines and shrubs with low-branching stems are the easiest plants to propagate this way. The new plants remain attached to the parent until they are sturdy enough to survive on their own. Once they're rooted, the new plants transplant easily.

**Use layering to give plants time before separation**   Layering involves pinning a branch to

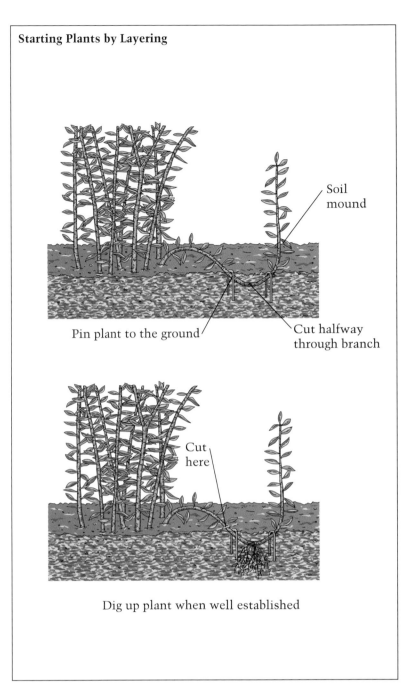

**Starting Plants by Layering**

Soil mound

Pin plant to the ground    Cut halfway through branch

Cut here

Dig up plant when well established

the ground and letting it take root before separating it from the parent plant. Begun in spring or early summer, the new plants get up to a full year of development before they are separated. The list that follows presents the steps in the layering process.

•Bend a pliable branch to the ground. Cut halfway through the branch on its underside and bury the cut section in a mound of soil. Use a turf pin or bent wire to anchor the branch on both sides of the soil mound. If the branch is long enough, layer it at several points in a serpentine pattern. New roots will form at each buried cut.

## Taking Hardwood Cuttings

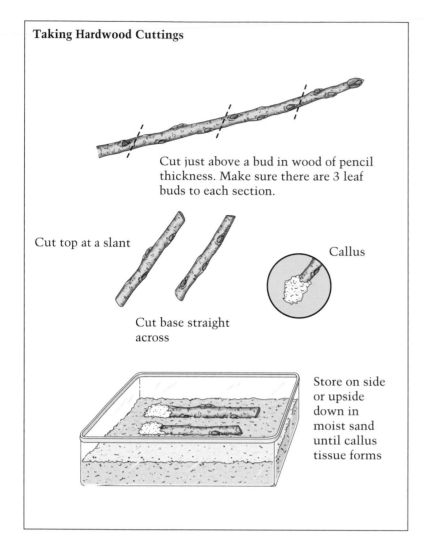

Cut just above a bud in wood of pencil thickness. Make sure there are 3 leaf buds to each section.

Cut top at a slant

Cut base straight across

Callus

Store on side or upside down in moist sand until callus tissue forms

## Taking Softwood Cuttings

Cut off 4"–8" of stem, including tip

Strip off ⅓ of lower leaves. Dip in rooting compound. Sink up to remaining leaves in sterile medium

Cover with plastic supported by sticks or straws

•Water the layered area during dry weather to keep the soil moist. Fence or flag off the area to prevent damage.

•Check the branch in a month for new growth. By fall, the sections should be sprouting strongly and rooted well enough to resist a gentle tug. In warm regions in fall, you can safely sever the cuttings from the parent and replant them. In areas of harsh winter weather, separate the layered cuttings in spring.

**Take cuttings to propagate shrubs and houseplants**   Shrubs, perennials, and annuals can all be propagated by cuttings. This is the best way to propagate most shrubs and many houseplants. Cuttings were the prime means of increasing nursery stock before the use of tissue culture and are still the preferred method of propagation for many plant species. The small sections severed from the plant become exact replicas of the parent.

**Take hardwood cuttings when plants are dormant**   Take hardwood cuttings from woody ornamentals, such as lilac and forsythia, during late fall or early winter. Each cutting will need at least three leaf buds. Find 8-inch sections of pencil-thick midbranch of the previous year's growth (see illustration). Make a slanting cut just above a bud. Cut the bottom of the cutting straight across, to distinguish top from bottom.

**Store hardwood cuttings at 32° to 40°F**   Place the cuttings upside down or on their sides in moist sand until calluses form over the cuts. Pull a cutting from the sand to check for callus formation every two weeks. Replace the cutting if callus tissue has not formed. Check a different cutting each time.

**Start hardwood cuttings in moist sand**   Once a callus has formed, dip the bottom cut in rooting hormone (available at most garden centers). Sink up to one third of the stem in moist sand. Keep the cuttings in a warm place. The air temperature should not drop below 70°F. Hardwood cuttings may take a year to become established.

**Take softwood cuttings when plants are actively growing** Take softwood cuttings from the pliable tips of woody plants. Make a slanting cut just below a leaf node, removing 4 to 8 inches of stem, including the tip and at least three nodes. Pinch off any flowers or fruit. Strip away one third of the leaves from the bottom of the cutting. Dip the base in rooting hormone, and sink the cutting up to the remaining leaves in a sterile soilless mix such as a packaged seed-starting mix.

**Cover softwood cuttings** Cover the cuttings with a clear plastic tent, supported by sticks or straws. Keep the soil moist, but not wet. If necessary, vent one edge of the plastic tent to allow excess moisture to escape. Softwood cuttings should root in two to six weeks, depending on the plant variety.

**Tug cuttings gently to determine when to pot** When cuttings are rooted well enough to resist a tug, transplant them into pots or flats. Place them in a bright spot out of direct sun for a few weeks, until they begin to grow strongly.

**Construct shields for tender transplants** Protect new plants when you plant them outside. Make a shield for newly set plants by cutting the top and bottom from a plastic jug, or by constructing a wire and plastic cage. Leave the top open to allow air movement. Cover the top of the cage only to protect the plants against frost. After a week or two, cut away the side of the cage opposite prevailing winds. Remove the cage one week later.

**Bury a jug to provide even watering** Poke several tiny holes in the base of a 1-gallon plastic jug. Sink the container several inches into the soil next to the tender plant. Keep the container filled with water.

## PRUNING TO MAKE PLANTS STRONG

Pruning keeps plants healthy and strong and is a vehicle for the gardener's art. Careful pruning trains plants into graceful and natural shapes.

**Trim evergreen shrubs from the bottom up** Make each cut beneath the shield of upper branches, working from the bottom to the upper levels of the shrub. This way each cut is hidden by the spread of the next layer of branches. The only fresh cuts exposed to view are those on the uppermost layer.

Ivy and other ground covers can also be pruned this way. Lift up the vines that are trailing across the path and reach underneath the top layer to cut. The cuts are hidden by the top layer, avoiding the ugly stubs that result from shearing at the edge.

**Prune spring-flowering shrubs shortly after blooming** Flowers for next season are formed on this year's wood. Later pruning will not hurt the shrub, but it will remove a portion of the year's growth, sacrificing next season's bloom.

**Trim summer-flowering shrubs when growth is just emerging** These shrubs set flowers on

*Shield newly set plants within clear plastic jugs with their tops and bottoms cut off.*

*To stimulate flowering, prune roses just above a five-leaflet leaf. A strong leaf indicates a strong bud at its base.*

the current season's growth, the new wood. To develop full shrubs and numerous flowers, prune in early spring, just as the plants are beginning to grow actively. In southern regions, prune in late fall or early spring. Late fall pruning in northern areas may stimulate a late flush of growth that would be highly susceptible to winter damage.

**Rejuvenate deciduous shrubs**   To rejuvenate shrubs, prune out approximately one third of the oldest branches at ground level. Trimming away old wood opens up the center of the plant to light and air and generally reduces overall shrub height, since the oldest branches are nearly always the tallest. Trimmed this way, a deciduous shrub will never develop overly woody, unattractive, and unproductive growth.

**Renew an overgrown hedge**   Some overgrown hedges can be cut back to within a few inches of the ground and will send out new growth. The success of this drastic pruning depends on the age, vitality, and variety of the plant.

**Make sculptures of overgrown shrubs**   Oversized, dense shrubs are often the result of years of neglect. Separate the outer layer of foliage and see what the stems look like inside. Some

of these shrubs are hiding beautifully shaped stems. Prune away much of the outer foliage and stems that hide the ones you want to expose. Once the shape of the shrub is established, keep it attractive with yearly pruning.

**Shear azaleas shortly after they have flowered**   Azaleas bloom both on terminal buds and on buds just beneath the bark all along the stem. Any of these buds can send out new growth. Shortly after an azalea has flowered, prune it back to maintain the desired compact shape. Dense new growth will emerge.

**Improve rhododendron flowers by removing spent blooms**   Rhododendrons bloom only on terminal buds, which form just below the previous year's blossom. To increase the vigor of the developing buds, remove the spent flower blossoms by gently twisting them from the branch, or allow the blossoms to drop and twist off the seedpods just as they start to form. Double flower production by pinching new growth back approximately 1 inch. New shoots will emerge, each bearing a flower bud.

**Prune roses just above a five-leaflet leaf**   Whether trimming a rose severely or simply removing a spent blossom, prune just above a five-leaflet leaf to encourage flowering. Make the cut as far back as desired to shape the bush. Choose an outward-facing leaf, and slant the angle of the cut away from the bush to open up the center and improve air circulation.

**Prune rambler roses heavily**   Rambler roses bloom only on year-old canes. Prune these rugged roses heavily each year (after they bloom) to keep a steady supply of blooming wood for the following season.

**Prune chrysanthemums to control blooming time**   For a mass of chrysanthemum blooms in fall, prevent the early flower buds from developing. Pinch off individual buds, clip back stems with pruning shears, or cut back foliage with hedge shears.

Usually, three trimmings are needed: the first when plants are 9 to 12 inches tall, the second at roughly 15 inches, and the third around early July. The timing of the last pinching may need to be adjusted to bring all the mums in one bed into bloom at the same time.

## Planting Ground Covers

The term ground cover describes the use of a plant, not its type. Some ground covers are low-growing evergreen or deciduous shrubs; others are herbaceous perennials or ornamental grasses. Most are available as actively growing container plants; a few come as field clumps or bare-root specimens. For planting methods, follow the directions for the specific plant type. Here are some simple tips to ensure success.

• Space ground-cover plants slightly closer together than their ultimate spread.

• Stagger hillside plantings. Set out plants on slopes so that those in one row will trap rainfall and loosened soil from the row above.

• To speed fill-in, use sod pins or bent metal clips to train the branches.

• Spread mulch around the plants and anchor it with netting to help retain moisture.

**Rejuvenate ground covers in spring** To rejuvenate woody ground covers, use pruning shears or hedge clippers to cut the plants back to near ground level. Some soft-stemmed varieties may be trimmed with a mower, using the highest possible mower setting and a very sharp blade. When mowing, use a bagger to collect clippings to avoid spreading diseases.

**Prune annuals, too** Because annuals grow rapidly throughout the season, they can easily become sprawling, lanky, or too dense. Pinch and prune them to bring them back to optimal condition.

**Pinch off spent flowers** Speed new flower production by snipping off the old flowers once they are past their prime. If the plants are too tall, pinch them farther back on the stem.

**Cut back sprawling plants** Trim overgrown annuals with hedge shears. Remove from one third to one half of the leaf surface if necessary to bring the plants back within the desired boundaries. Many lank and unattractive annuals will put out a new flush of growth and blooms after being cut back.

**Rejuvenate neglected plants** Use pruning shears to clip off blossoms and 1 or 2 inches of foliage when annuals start to look neglected.

Instead of struggling to maintain flowering, the plant will devote its resources to producing new, lush growth. Replace the plants that fail to revive.

**Root-prune large plants before moving them** Root-prune from 1 to 12 months before moving the plant. The larger and slower-growing the plant, the longer the interval should be between root pruning and moving. Use a sharp spade to slice through the soil at the drip line of the plant. Make a second cut a little farther out. Remove the wedge of soil. Dig down additional spade depths in the same manner, checking root size. Move in toward the trunk a few inches and repeat the procedure. Continue until you reach finger-sized roots. This will be the approximate outer edge of the root mass that's needed to sustain the plant. Remaining this distance from the main trunk, use a spade to sever the roots in a circle all around the plant. Root pruning forces the growth of additional feeder roots.

**Dig up the plant** Spread a tarp on which to pile soil. Starting at the drip line, cut straight down with a sharp spade. Work around the plant, then move in toward the main trunk until you reach a mass of new root growth or

*Trim soft-stemmed ground covers with a mower set on the highest height setting. These St. John's worts (Hypericum) were pruned this way.*

## Working With the Soil

Check the soil conditions of different parts of the landscape and get to know how these conditions affect the plants.

• Long-term plantings, such as trees and shrubs, may be struggling in compacted soil, which limits air and water availability. Use a plug-type aerator once or twice a year to open up the soil.

• Years of growing annuals in the same spot may have depleted the nutrients and organic matter in once-rich soils. Mix compost into the bed before spring planting.

• The removal of shade trees or screening shrubs may be exposing planted soils to baking sunlight or wind and rain erosion. To protect soils from the elements, break up the crust and add mulch.

• Lime leached from building foundations or other such surfaces may change the soil pH. Test the soil, using a soil test kit (available from an extension service or garden center) or have the soil tested by a qualified professional. Amend the soil according to the test results.

finger-sized roots (depending on whether roots have been pruned). Continue to dig straight down one spade depth at a time, shaving excess soil away with the spade little by little. Use the spade to cut straight across at the bottom of the rootball.

**Wrap the soil ball with burlap**   Anchor burlap around the soil ball, using long thin nails with wide heads (pinning nails). Start pinning on one side and then stretch the burlap around and underneath the plant. Rock the rootball slightly to one side by pushing carefully on the ball itself. Using the trunk or branches as a lever may break up the ball. Continue pinning, then secure the burlap with twine for added support of the soil ball.

**Lift the plant from the hole**   Slip a piece of heavy canvas, cardboard, or chicken wire under the rootball for added support as you lift it from the hole.

**Move the plant to its new site**   If the plant is too heavy to carry to the planting site, ease it onto a board placed over the top of a wagon, wheelbarrow, or garden cart. Lay planks over

any turf areas on the way to the planting site to prevent wheel damage.

## PROTECTING PLANTS

Plants often need protection from the elements, animals, or other plants. The need to provide protection can sometimes be avoided by selecting plants that are adapted to your region. But there are always a few delicate princesses that are worth fussing over.

**Apply preemergence control to prevent weeds**   Several preemergence herbicides are labeled for use around trees, shrubs, and flowers; use them to prevent the growth of annual weeds. Apply the preemergence herbicide after planting. Water it in well but do not rake or till the soil. The herbicide binds to the first inch or so of earth, and prevents seeds from germinating there. Tilling or digging dilutes the herbicide and allows weed seeds to grow. The control will last about six weeks, longer in dry areas.

**Mulch after planting**   Mulch new plantings with 3 inches of organic material or with landscape fabric covered by a thin layer of organic matter. When weeds break through the mulch, pull them at an angle, slanting away from desirable plants, to avoid damaging tender roots.

**Protect delicate plants from cold**   Cover plants with landscape fabric when frosts are predicted, or move them to a more sheltered area of the garden. Shrubs that bloom in early spring may lose blossoms to frosts. If blooms appear on the lower and inner branches, but not at the tips and tops, frost damage is usually the cause.

**Build shields of burlap or landscape fabric**   Hardy plants can often withstand winter cold but suffer dehydration from drying winds. Broadleaf and needled evergreens release moisture the year around—moisture that cannot be replaced when the soil is frozen. Protect vulnerable plants from wind and sun with temporary fences and covers of landscape fabric. Spraying plants with an antitranspirant also helps retain moisture.

**Shelter plants with perforated or vented covers**   With no air flow from the outside, some protective covers can become mini-hothouses on sunny days. The warm, humid conditions beneath the covers may trick the plants into sprouting when the temperature is still well below freezing. Use a pencil to poke several rings of small holes in the top and middle of cardboard and polystyrene covers. Some covers have built-in vents. You may need to open or close these as often as several times a day or night to prevent inappropriate warming and possible unseasonable sprouting.

**Water plants during the winter**   When winter moisture is sparse, plants need supplemental watering, even in northern regions. Start root feeders or slowly trickling hoses as soon in the day as the soil becomes sufficiently warmed and will absorb moisture. Stop watering an hour or two before temperatures drop in the evening.

**Remove winter coverings gradually**   Remove protective winter mulches an inch or so at a time in early spring, as the weather begins to warm. Complete the removal over a period of at least two weeks or as much as a month, depending on the weather conditions.

**Remove snow**   Although mounded snow can make an excellent winter mulch, it can also crush and break branches. Wet snows are much heavier than dry ones and more likely to cause damage. To remove a dangerous weight of snow, support the weight of the branch and gently brush away the snow with a broom. Don't try to shake off the snow or to scrape it away with a rake or shovel.

Shrubs that are liable to being spread apart by a burden of snow can be bound with twine in the fall to support them against the weight.

**Prevent mouse damage**   Mice nest under the cozy mulch of perennial beds and nibble on tender plants. Wait until the ground is solidly frozen before applying winter mulches.

**Protect tender bulbs**   To keep mice away, encase bulbs in wire cages at the time of planting, leaving an opening at the top for the leaves and flowers to emerge.

**Identify problem insects**   When insect damage occurs, consult qualified nursery professionals or reference books (see page 92) to identify the perpetrators and to provide solutions. If no insects are visible, they are probably night feeders. Search for them near the plants with a flashlight after dark.

Place one or more of the insects in a clear, sealed container for examination. If the insect is identified as one that can cause damage, follow the treatment plan recommended in the reference book or by the nursery.

*Remove snow burdens to keep the weight from breaking or deforming branches.*

*Top: Each spot on this leaf is a separate infection. The fungi that cause the spots make spores that create new infections. Protect the leaf from new infections with fungicide sprays.*

*Bottom: Spray to reach every part of the plant. Repeat the application to control insects that were still eggs at the original spray.*

**Follow up with repeat treatments** Many insects are susceptible to pesticides only during one part of their life cycle. When you spray, you may kill the adults but the eggs may be unaffected by the pesticide and hatch in the next several days or weeks. Repeat treatments will prevent successive invasions.

**Maximize spray effectiveness** Always follow directions precisely and use sufficient spray pressure to cover all parts of the plant well, including the bottom sides of the leaves and inside tightly bunched growth. Spray until the leaves begin to drip. Notice where the insects congregate and spray those parts well. For example, mites usually stay on the underside of leaves; spray from the bottom up to wet them. Aphids often cluster on new growth; spray tips of branches to control these insects.

**Make a barricade of snail bait** Snails spend the day under cover, often in dense ground covers. Place a line of snail bait between areas like this and the plants you wish to protect. If you don't know where the snails come from, surround the plants you want to protect with a line of snail bait. Renew the snail bait every two weeks.

**Create sticky barriers**  Wrap the main branches of shrubs with tree wrap or cheesecloth. Spread on the wrap a layer of latex or some other sticky substance intended to stop bugs. The sticky stuff will trap insects as they try to crawl up to the foliage. (Products for creating sticky barriers are available at most nurseries.)

**Handle disease problems promptly**  Many plant diseases are local infections that attack one leaf or one spot on a leaf at a time. The disease organism (usually a fungus) then makes spores that attack other leaves or other spots. A timely spray can prevent this cycle of infection and sporing from building to a crescendo that destroys the whole plant.

**Clean up plant debris**  A proper fall cleanup, coupled with cold winter temperatures, can eliminate many disease problems. Since disease organisms develop within the fallen leaves of infected plants, rake up and dispose of this material. Do not use it as mulch or add it to the regular compost pile. If there is a large supply of diseased material, establish a special compost pile, turning it frequently to keep the temperature high enough to destroy most of the disease organisms. Use the humus from this special pile for fill in unplanted areas or around plants of different types than the diseased ones, plants that are not susceptible to the particular disease. Where landfills will accept yard wastes, diseased material can be disposed of with other trash.

**Apply fungicides to protect new foliage**  Most fungicides inhibit the germination of fungus spores, preventing diseases from spreading. A plant is protected wherever the fungicide has been sprayed, and the protection may last for several weeks. New growth will not be protected, however. Do touch-up sprayings to cover the new foliage with fungicide. Spray as often as necessary, depending on how fast the plant is growing. This is especially important with diseases that primarily attack new growth, such as powdery mildew.

**Keep water off the foliage**  When disease is active in a group of plants, water only the soil around the plants, using slowly running water from a hose. Overhead watering spreads disease organisms from the infected plants,

## Glossary of Nursery Terms

**Bud**  A small swelling or projection on a plant, from which a flower, leaf, or shoot develops. A growth bud is the point from which new foliage or a shoot emerges. It may be at the tip of the stem (a terminal bud) or on the side of the stem (a lateral bud). A flower bud is the growth point for a blossom. *Budding* refers to a method of propagation similar to grafting.

**Bud union**  The place on a plant where the bud or actively growing portion of one plant type is grafted onto the stock of another plant. For roses, the bud union is the point where a hybrid rose variety is grafted onto the rootstock of a hardier rose variety.

**Bulb**  A thick and rounded underground stem composed of fleshy scales. The outer scales dry, forming a papery covering; inner scales store food and protect the developing plant inside.

**Corm**  Like a bulb, a corm is an underground stem capable of producing roots, leaves, and flowers. Food is stored in the solid center tissue of a corm, rather than in scales.

**Graft**  The point on a plant where grafting has taken place.

**Grafting**  A method of plant propagation in which a section of one plant (called the scion) is inserted into the branch or stem of another plant (called the stock).

**Herbaceous plant**  A plant with soft, nonwoody tissue. Usually dies back to the ground each year. Perennial herbaceous plants re-sprout the next year from the portion below ground.

**Invasive**  Plants that increase in size so rapidly that they extend into surrounding spots, intruding on other plants or property.

**Layering**  A method of propagation in which a branch is pegged to the ground at one point. Roots will form at that point.

**Puddling**  A method of watering a new planting. After the plant is positioned in the planting hole and the hole filled partway with soil, water is poured to the top and allowed to soak in. The hole is then filled with soil and the plant watered thoroughly.

**Rhizome**  A stem that grows horizontally along or under the soil surface. New plants can form at the joints.

**Rooting hormone**  A product in powder form that contains growth hormone and sometimes vitamins. The ends of cuttings are dipped in the compound before being placed in soil. Also called rooting compound.

**Rootstock**  The portion of a budded or grafted plant that provides the root system and may provide a part of the stem.

**Scion**  The segment of a plant that is grafted onto another plant or plant portion.

**Tuber**  A thickened underground stem from which a plant grows. Tubers are similar to rhizomes but are usually shorter and thicker.

splashing them onto the foliage of uninfected plants or to the ground, where they may be absorbed through plant roots.

**Cut back on fertilizer when plants are diseased**  Tender, rapidly growing tissue is the most susceptible to disease. Stop or cut back on fertilizer applications until the plants show no further disease symptoms.

# Bringing In the Harvest

*Following the tips from the food production professionals will lead to better plant selection; sound planning; the optimal level of production; and ultimately, to delicious-tasting fruits and vegetables. The tips will also help you cut the time and energy needed to make it all happen.*

Professionals in food production—farmers, orchardists, truck gardeners, and pick-your-own operators—have developed techniques to obtain the maximum production from their fields and the fastest and easiest methods of producing it. Researchers have developed varieties for better fruiting, increased resistance to insects and diseases, and improved adaptability to soil and climate. For small gardens and intensively farmed areas, they have developed dwarf and semidwarf fruit trees and compact, bush-type vegetables.

Commercial growers strive for large quantities of top-quality, marketable produce. Home gardeners seek the same quality, and high yields. But their motivations are primarily the taste of fresh produce and growing plants that beautify the landscape. The heaviest harvest may not be the best harvest for the home gardener. The trick in home gardens is to raise the right amount of each crop, within the space available, in the most efficient manner.

All plants need some care. Decide how much time can be devoted to crop plants and raise those whose requirements will not be too demanding. If vacation or other travel plans mean a long period away from home, choose crops that can be picked before or after that time.

*An attractive, delicious, and plentiful harvest is no accident. Professional growers rely on years of experience.*

## GROWING FRUIT TREES

Fruit trees demand attention: periodic pruning, supplemental food and water, and prevention and control of insects and diseases, as well as harvesting. In return, they provide healthful, tasty produce and add beauty to the landscape.

**Provide for pollination needs**  Some fruit trees are self-pollinating; others need a compatible variety close by—usually no farther away than 100 feet—for cross-pollination.

If space allows for only one tree and it is not self-pollinating, check the neighborhood for compatible pollinators. Hang a water-filled bucket of blooming branches cut from the pollinator tree in the branches of the blooming tree that needs pollination. Alternatively, graft a branch from a compatible variety onto the tree that needs cross-pollination. In such grafting, a bud or branch of a compatible variety is inserted into the trunk or a main branch of the tree. Consult a nursery professional for advice on selecting compatible varieties and the grafting process.

**Respond appropriately in critical periods**
Fruit trees must have sufficient water during flowering and when harvest is near and the fruit is developing rapidly. If the rainfall is insufficient during these two critical periods, water the soil to a depth of 8 to 12 inches.

To test for moisture, insert a soil probe or porous stick to this depth. Feel the soil the probe or stick brings to the surface and check for the clinging soil particles and dark discoloration caused by soil moisture. Provide water if it's needed.

**Water trees before the ground freezes**
Young trees are especially susceptible to harsh, drying winter air, which draws moisture from exposed plant surfaces. If the trees need water, water them before the ground freezes, so the roots can sustain the tree through the winter. If there is little winter snow or rainfall, water again during warm spells when the soil is able to absorb water.

**Apply fertilizer in late fall or winter**  After trees are dormant, usually in late fall, apply a complete fruit-tree fertilizer, which contains nitrogen, phosphorus, and potash in the proper proportions for both growth and fruit production. Spread the material evenly over the soil surface or make an in-ground application, drilling evenly spaced holes throughout the root zone of the tree. (See page 25 for tips on this procedure.) In regions where trees grow actively the year around, apply fertilizer in late winter, using the same procedure. Follow these suggestions for individual fruits.

•Most apples are fairly heavy feeders and benefit from yearly fertilizer applications.

•Pears use less fertilizer than apples; extremely lush growth promotes fire blight. Annually, apply a balanced fertilizer containing approximately ⅕ pound of nitrogen per year of tree age, up to a maximum of 4 pounds.

•Fertilize cherries only when slowed growth or light-colored foliage signals a lack of necessary nutrients.

•Citrus trees grow best with annual applications of fertilizer in January or February.

•Figs seldom need fertilizer.

*Nurseries stock a wide variety of fruit trees that are suited to local conditions.*

## Pruning For a Bountiful Crop

A fruit tree is pruned to open up its interior. An open center lets sunlight penetrate, which improves fruit production and allows easier picking. Although the pruning techniques are the same for fruit trees as for other trees, more branches are removed from the inside of fruit trees and the pruner concentrates more on the productivity of individual branches than on the overall shape of the tree.

Pruning methods vary according to cultivar and regional growing conditions. Some fruit trees need hard pruning; others, very little. Use these general rules as guidelines.

**Apple**   Bear on long-lived spurs (see illustration below), which are short, squat twigs that line the branches. Spurs can bear fruit for 10 years or more; however, spur growth doesn't begin until 3 to 5 years after a tree is planted.

**Apricot**   Bear on the previous season's wood, with the bulk of production on four-year-old spurs, which fall off after bearing. Heavy pruning is needed to open up the center and allow light into the interior.

**Citrus**   Need little pruning. Remove suckers and shoots growing inward at the junction of the branches.

**Fig**   With severe pruning a fig tree can be kept as low as 5 to 6 feet tall. Severe pruning is necessary to prevent frost damage, except in the very warmest regions. Figs bear on wood one year old and older.

**Nectarine**   Produce fruit on the previous season's growth. Trim off one half of this year's new growth for a good crop next year.

**Peach**   Prune to maintain a low head with an open center and a shape that will encourage fruit production and reduce wind damage. Prune established peach trees quite severely; as growth slows, so does production.

**Pear**   Keep low to the ground—with lowest branches 1½ feet above the soil line. The low canopy protects the trunk and helps avoid sunscald and fire blight.

**Plum**   Mature trees require only a little pruning to control height; remove deadwood and crossing limbs. Japanese plum varieties bear on twigs and spurs of new wood. European varieties bear on spurs of old wood.

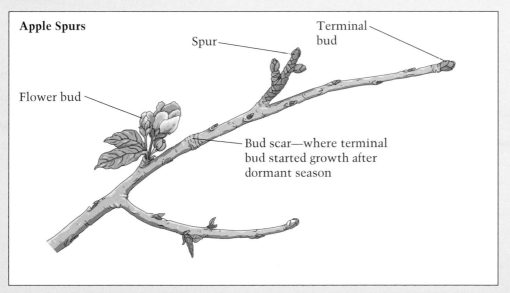

**Apple Spurs**

Terminal bud

Spur

Flower bud

Bud scar—where terminal bud started growth after dormant season

•Peaches, plums, apricots, and nectarines are relatively light feeders, responding to excessive fertilizer or especially rich soil with beautiful foliage and no fruit.

**Shield blossoms from late spring frosts**   Protect tender blossoms on fruit trees from late-season frosts by covering the tree with landscape fabric, old blankets, or sheeting. Spread the covering early enough in the day to trap a little heat next to the foliage, but not so early that excess heat builds up. Remove the covering the following day, after the sun has burned the frost off the ground.

Alternatively, cover the tree with a clear plastic tarp and place a 25- to 50-watt light

*Cover fruit trees to protect the blossoms from frost damage.*

bulb in the center of the tree. (Use an extension cord from the nearest power source to illuminate the bulb.) Turn the light on when the temperature drops to 34°F. The heat from the bulb is trapped within the tarp and will keep the blossoms from freezing even if temperatures drop as low as 20°F.

**Time sprays carefully**   If you adopt a season-long preventive spray program, follow the label directions to time the applications appropriately. Timing is critical and dependent on the growth stage of the tree. A preventive program usually begins with a dormant spray and resumes after the blossoms drop (to avoid killing pollinating bees) and continues until the fruit is half grown.

**Improve spray timing with pheromone traps**   Pheromone traps, which use a natural hormonal stimulant to lure insects inside, can help you fine-tune the timing of spray applications. A coddling moth pheromone trap, for example, will let you know when the coddling moth, which lays eggs that become apple worms, becomes active. When moths begin appearing in the traps, apply the first spray.

**Trap insects and worms**   Certain insects, such as aphids and whiteflies, are attracted to

bright yellow. Other insects, such as apple maggot flies, are attracted to a red ball in the center of a yellow rectangle. Coat 10-inch by 10-inch traps of either type with a sticky substance. When the insects land, they become trapped and die. Use several traps in each tree.

Trap worms and other insects that crawl up trunks by circling the trunk with a sticky trap. Wrap a strip of tree wrap around the trunk of the tree firmly enough to be secure, but not tightly enough to restrict growth. Spread the surface of the fabric with sticky material. Remove and dispose of the fabric when it becomes filled or the sight becomes offensive. If the damaging insects are still active, put out a fresh trap.

**Wrap the trunks with aluminum foil**   Trunk-climbing insects can be discouraged with a broad section of aluminum foil—they will slide on its slick surface. Tightly wrap the trunk with a wide strip.

**Treat borers at once**   Borers are a common problem on peach, apple, plum, and cherry trees. Borers can seriously weaken and even kill a tree. They burrow into the trunk and main branches, damaging the water and nutrient passages that link the roots and foliage. Examine the main trunk and large branches for

## Harvesting the Fruit

Unless the crop is so light that you can carry it in your hands, pad the basket you put picked fruit into. Use soft cloth for padding, especially if you are using a wire fruit picker. Examine fruits closely, and separate those with minor blemishes for early use.

Most fruits can be picked within a day or two of the prime ripening period. Fruit should be firm, yet yield lightly to the touch. Pick fruit that is past its prime, regardless of whether it is edible. Overripe fruit attracts insects that will also attack the developing fruit.

**Apples**   Pick apples for immediate use when the aroma is good and the colors have turned over most of the fruit. Pick apples going into storage for winter use as soon as they begin to ripen.

Hold each apple firmly in one hand and the tip of the branch in the other. Twist the apple and lift slightly to remove it from the tree. Keep the stem intact to prevent early rotting. Take care not to damage leaves and developing fruit buds.

**Cherries**   The sugar content of cherries increases greatly over the last few days of ripening, so fully colored cherries will be much sweeter than less ripe ones. For immediate use, gently pull ripe cherries away from the pits and stems. This eliminates the pitting process. However, if the cherries will be used even a day later, keep stems intact when picking. Open wounds on the fruit brown quickly, so remove pits and stems just before using the fruit. Set cherries into containers when picking; dropping causes bruises.

**Citrus**   The longer citrus fruit stays on the tree after maturity, the shorter its storage life. Wear gloves to pick citrus fruits; the rinds are delicate and easily broken. Clip each fruit from the tree then place it gently into a container.

**Figs**   Pick figs when they are fully ripe. They are bitter before that point, but then deteriorate quickly if left on the tree. Taste a few to test the flavor and ripeness.

**Pears**   Pears that ripen on the tree have a gritty texture. When pears begin to turn from green to yellow, test a few by gently tipping the stem end toward the branch. When the stem comes off easily, the pear is ready for picking.

Pick pears gently to avoid bruising. Bruised spots soon rot. Wrap each fruit in soft paper and keep it at 70°F to finish ripening. Eat pears when the color reaches an even yellow and the flesh is firm to the touch.

**Peaches**   Ripe peaches release from the branch easily. If the stem resists, and must be torn away, the peach is not ripe enough for picking. Cup each peach gently, lift it up and twist it slightly. Avoid bruising the flesh or tearing stems. Set the fruit into containers; do not drop them in.

**Plums**   Because plums improve in flavor while hanging on the tree, store them there when weather permits. Ripe plums spring back quickly when poked lightly with a finger. Pick them just before using.

Remove plums with a slight twist. Hold each fruit gently to prevent bruising and twist it slightly to separate it from the tree. Hold the branch with your other hand as you remove each plum. Set in containers; dropping causes bruises, which will soon rot.

*Apples are ready for picking when the color has turned.*

*Check citrus fruit for ripeness carefully—the rinds break easily.*

signs of sawdust or small spots of oozing sap. If you see either of these signs, apply a borer control spray to the trunk and main branches, according to the label instructions.

**Apply fungicides before disease arrives**  Unlike insecticides, which are most effective when insects are already present, fungicides protect plants against disease, preventing disease spores from invading the tissues. Ask local nursery professionals for disease spray schedules for your area and follow them closely. Timing is critical for effective control. As new growth appears, repeat treatments are necessary to protect it.

**Clean up the area around the fruit trees**
Since disease organisms need time to develop and spread, removing debris and fallen fruit regularly will eliminate many disease problems. Clean up weeds and debris from the area beneath and surrounding fruit trees. Remove and dispose of weak and damaged branches.

**Never work on wet fruit trees**  Postpone pruning or picking when the foliage is wet or damp. Disease organisms spread more quickly in moist conditions.

## GROWING SMALL FRUITS AND BERRIES

The small fruits and berries most frequently grown in home gardens are blackberries, raspberries, grapes, and strawberries. These plants will thrive just about anywhere. Moreover, huge spaces and massive plantings are not required to enjoy these fruits fresh-picked.

**Mulch berries**  Blackberries, raspberries, and strawberries are shallow rooted. Spread a 2- to 3-inch-deep layer of mulch around the base of each plant to protect the roots. Shallow-cultivate only; deep hoeing will cut roots and limit production.

**Feed before growth starts in spring**  In late winter or early spring, apply slow-release nitrogen as part of a complete, granular fertilizer that also contains phosphorus and potash. Spread the granules evenly over the surface of the plant bed. Water lightly to wash the fertilizer into the soil, where it can be absorbed by the roots.

**Prune everbearing raspberries for multiple crops**  After the season's first flush of fruit on everbearing raspberries, cut off the canes that bore the fruit. Tie up the remaining young canes; these will fruit in the fall. After the fall harvest, trim off only the portions of the canes that produced fruit. The remaining portion will bear the spring crop.

**Protect ripening grapes from birds and bees**  Birds will pick and eat the ripening grapes or peck holes in them. Bees will make a

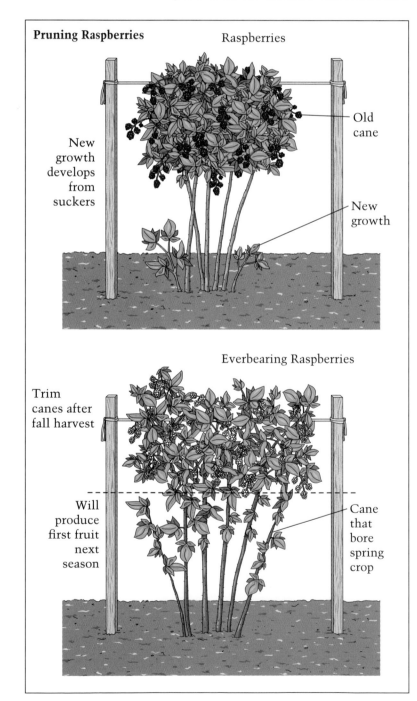

**Pruning Raspberries**

Raspberries

New growth develops from suckers

Old cane

New growth

Everbearing Raspberries

Trim canes after fall harvest

Will produce first fruit next season

Cane that bore spring crop

small hole to drain out the grape flesh, leaving an empty skin to wither on the vine. Since grapes don't need direct sunlight to develop fruit color, slip a brown paper bag over each bunch when the fruit is half grown. Secure the bags to the vines with soft plastic or cloth ties. Don't use plastic bags, or the fruit will rot. If the weather is wet, check inside the paper bags frequently to be sure no rot has begun.

**Choose certified, virus-free strawberry plants** Avoid virus problems by using resistant varieties. Examine plants closely, rejecting those that show mold, are poorly developed, or have black or brown discoloration around the crown. Keep the plants cool and moist until you are ready to plant them; refrigerate if necessary.

**Nip selectively to boost strawberry production** For long-term beds nip off the first-year blossoms and runners. This prevents the plants from channeling energy to fruit production. The root system and foliage can then develop more fully, strengthening the plants to support heavy crops in the future.

**Plant strawberries through weed-blocking fabric** For the best weed control, before planting cover the soil with weed-blocking fabric, securing it at the edges of the rows or mounds. Cut a slit or an *X*, then fold back the fabric and carefully set the plant.

**Plant alpine strawberries for children** Alpine strawberries, available as seeds from several seed catalogs, are usually grown as ornamentals. They do not produce runners, so are well behaved as a bed or border plant. Although their fruit is sweet and tasty, it is small and sparse compared to other strawberries. But children love poking through a border or bed of alpine strawberries, looking for the berries.

**Fertilize strawberries after harvest** After the final picking each season, apply a slow-release, complete fertilizer with more phosphorus or phosphorus and potash in it than nitrogen—such as a 5-10-5 or 8-10-10 formula. This will strengthen roots and stems.

**Rejuvenate old beds when production drops** When the strawberry bed is bearing well, for the most part, but a few plants are declining,

sever the unproductive plants from their strong runners. Remove the severed plants and allow the runners to fill in the bed. When the entire bed is declining, cut back the plants to about 3 inches, fertilize, and water them.

**Protect strawberries from birds** Prevent birds from eating the ripening strawberries by constructing a string-and-stick framework and covering it with netting. Make the frame high enough so the netting will be several inches above the berries. Some birds will stand on the netting, using their weight to press the netting down to where they can peck at berries through it. Staple one edge of the netting to a light board or rod. Fasten the other edge to the ground. To work on the berries, throw the pole back across the bed. Replace it when you are through working.

**Control snails and slugs from the outset** Keep snails and slugs from entering planting beds by using a barrier of snail pellets, liquid snail bait, or copper stripping. Around the bed scatter snail pellets or make a line of liquid snail bait. Add new pellets or refresh the liquid line every two weeks. If the beds are raised and have a wood border, nail a copper strip to the wood, completely encircling the bed (see page 92 for sources of copper strips). Snails and slugs will not cross the copper, since it gives them a galvanic shock.

*Pinch blossoms and runners off strawberry plants the first year. This will result in more and larger berries in future years. If you can't wait, plant extras to have berries for this year.*

## GROWING VEGETABLES

Vegetable gardening can be successful in plots large or small. Choose the size of the planting area and the kinds of plants to match the time available for planting, maintenance, and harvest, and for your family's taste.

Certain vegetables have very specific needs. These are discussed in later sections. General maintenance and care procedures, including how to handle insect and disease problems, are also outlined.

**Soap fingernails before getting dirty**   Dig fingernails into a soft bar of soap before working in the garden. Nails will wash clean afterward.

**Inspect plants regularly for insects**   The key to successful insect control is early intervention—before the insects become established and before they do much damage. Look under leaves and inside dense growth. Carry a 5-power hand magnifying lens for a better look and a jar for samples. Identify insects correctly

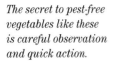

*The secret to pest-free vegetables like these is careful observation and quick action.*

with the help of nursery personnel or problem solver books (see page 92). If a control spray is recommended, follow the usage instructions carefully.

**Use floating row covers to keep out flying insects**   Floating row covers—lightweight fabrics that don't need staking—are often used to protect plants from late spring frosts. Row covers also keep flying insects from reaching young vegetables. Weight down one side of the fabric with rocks or dirt; the other side, with a long board. Move the board and throw back the row cover to work the bed, then replace it when you are through. Remove the row cover when hot weather begins.

**Deter cutworms**   Cut away the tops and bottoms of gallon-sized plastic jugs. Sink these containers one half to three quarters of the way into the ground around small seedlings. The underground portion serves as a barrier, keeping cutworms from snipping off the stems.

*A mulch around the plants all but eliminates weeding at the same time as it benefits the plants and conserves water.*

**Prevent borer attacks**  Wrap strips of aluminum foil around the stems of plants susceptible to borer attacks, such as squash and melon. Borers tunnel into the stem, often spreading disease organisms, and weaken or kill the plant. Wrap the foil firmly, but not so tight to prevent growth. Extend the foil wrap from the lowest leaves to 1 or 2 inches below the soil level to form a barrier.

**Select disease-resistant varieties**  Many problems can be avoided by choosing plants that have been bred to resist certain disease organisms. Check plant labels or seek recommendations from professionals for the best regionally adapted varieties.

**Lay fabric or a mulch to control weeds**  To prevent weeds from getting started, spread weed control fabric across beds before planting. With a knife, cut X's to plant seedlings or long slits to sow rows of seeds. Weed control fabric is sufficiently porous to let air and rain through, but tight enough to keep weeds from sprouting. As an alternative to fabric, lay a mulch of any available organic material, such as sawdust, straw, or compost. Put on enough so that the mulch will be about 3 inches deep when it settles.

**Set asparagus roots in trenches**  Dig wide trenches, 6 to 8 inches deep, with a slightly raised center ridge. Set the crown of the plant on the ridge, with the buds pointing up, and spread the roots so they radiate around the crown. Cover with 2 to 3 inches of soil. When the shoots poke through, add soil gently from the sides, repeating the process until the trench is level with the surrounding soil.

**Harvest asparagus with a sharp knife**  Cut at soil surface to avoid damaging the crowns and the tender tips that have not yet emerged. When the crop slows, usually after about six weeks, stop picking and let the ferns grow.

**Remove asparagus top growth**  After the first heavy frost, cut back the fernlike top growth to ground level and remove it from the area. Clearing away the foliage will prevent insects and diseases from overwintering.

**Force early rhubarb growth**  For a spring harvest, force a plant or two. As soon as the soil warms, set an open-ended, 18-inch-tall box or circle of plastic or wood over the plant. Harvest the tender, pink stalks as they stretch for light.

**Harvest rhubarb by twisting stalks**  Grasp a single stalk, and twist it lightly out of the crown. Cutting below the soil surface may damage developing stalks; cutting above the soil surface leaves entry sites for insects and diseases. Pick the mature, outside stalks first to stimulate further growth. Dispose of these stalks if they have become too woody to use.

**Plant garlic cloves anytime**   Separate cloves at any time of year and place them 2 inches deep in any soil. Fall-planted garlic will mature over the winter for spring use.

**Harvest young garlic shoots as well as bulbs**   Harvest the actively growing young shoots, which have a mild, delicate flavor, to mince for salads. After the tops die down, dig up the entire clump with a spade. Dry the bulbs before using them.

**Rotate tomatoes**   Even when using disease-resistant varieties, choose a new location for tomatoes each season. Set the plants as far as possible from the previous location, far enough so that there's no possibility of the roots reaching into the previous site. For best results, select different varieties each year, going back to an old favorite every fourth season.

**Maintain stable moisture levels**   Water is critical for the first five to six weeks after transplanting tomatoes and again during fruit production. Blossom end rot will result if water levels fluctuate during fruit development. Install drip irrigation, or punch several tiny holes in the bottom of a gallon container and sink it 1 to 2 inches into the soil near the stem of the plant. Keep the container filled with water. The tomato plant will draw moisture from the soil as it needs it.

**Speed tomato ripening**   When the fruit reach a good size, firmly grasp the main stem of the plant and pull it upward until a few roots snap. The plant will be threatened by the stress and direct energy to ripening in an effort to reproduce itself.

**Mound soil around pepper stems**   Although they look sturdy, pepper plants of all varieties have brittle stems and are easily damaged by winds or heavy rains. Form a 6- to 8-inch soil mound around the base of the plants to provide extra support.

**Harvesting Asparagus**

Harvest with sharp knife at soil surface

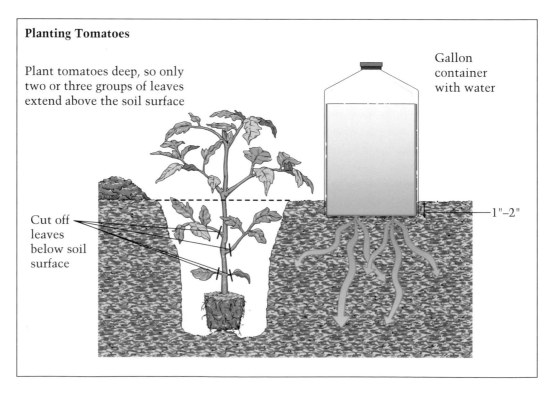

**Planting Tomatoes**

Plant tomatoes deep, so only two or three groups of leaves extend above the soil surface

Gallon container with water

Cut off leaves below soil surface

1"–2"

*Plant corn in blocks. Stagger planting times for a longer harvest.*

**Snip ripe peppers with scissors or shears** Cut off the peppers; pulling may injure the delicate roots and stop production. Frequent picking encourages fruit set.

**Plant corn in blocks** Ensure pollination and protect corn from wind damage by planting it in blocks of short rows. Space plants 18 inches apart in rows 18 inches apart. Three or four rows are needed to ensure pollination. Thin plants as needed. Depending on the variety, corn plants may spread 1½ feet to 4 feet. Crowded corn yields less.

**Keep corn rows weed-free** Corn cannot withstand weed competition. Mulch, or use a hoe or cultivator to scratch the upper inch or two of soil, which will remove the weeds and prevent the soil from crusting. Continue to shallow-cultivate until the corn is half grown. Once the plants are well developed, they will shade out the weeds. Hoe extra soil up against the base of the plants on each side of the rows to preserve moisture and strengthen roots.

**Plant corn in warm weather** Wait until the soil warms to plant, normally a week or two after the usual frost-free date. Later corn will catch up with plants started too soon.

**Destroy cornstalks in the fall** Dead stalks may harbor the larvae of the European corn borer. Unless the stalks are destroyed, the larvae will overwinter in them, and adults will emerge in spring.

**Make successive plantings** Corn earworms and certain other corn-damaging insects are normally active for only a short period. Make three or four separate plantings at two-week intervals to avoid losing a complete crop to any one insect infestation.

**Deter animal raiders** Erect a 4-foot wire mesh fence leaving the top 8 to 12 inches unsupported. Stretch the fence around the entire corn patch. Raccoons and other animals won't venture on to the unsteady top section. To keep animals from burrowing under the fence, turn the bottom foot of the fence out on the ground and pile soil on it. Burrowing animals will try to dig under the vertical part of the fence and be stopped by the horizontal portion. They won't try to back up and dig under that portion, too.

**Harvest when the silks are brown**   On ripe ears the silks are brown and feel damp to the touch and the tops of the cobs are round, not pointed. Poke a plump kernel with a fingernail; if milky fluid spurts out, the ear is ready.

**Blanch cauliflower**   As soon as cauliflower heads begin to form, pull the outer leaves over the developing head and secure the leaves with a soft tie. Allow enough room within the covering of leaves for air to circulate and the head to develop. Protected from the sun, the maturing cauliflower turns from dull yellow to white.

**Pinch off the growing tip of brussels sprouts**   When sprout plants reach 15 to 20 inches, stop top growth. Pinching off the tops will produce sprouts that are more uniform and ready for harvest earlier.

**Reap a double harvest of broccoli**   With a sharp knife, cut off the main head of broccoli when it matures, leaving the rest of the plant in place. A second crop will develop from the side shoots. Pick these small heads regularly to keep the plant producing.

**Keep cabbage heads from cracking**   Once cabbage heads are hard, either cut them for immediate use or stop them from growing so they don't burst. To stop growth, twist or jerk the plant to break off some of the feeder roots. The head will stay green and healthy, but growth will stop.

**Harvest brussels sprouts from the bottom of the stalk first**   Harvest sprouts neatly, picking first the mature sprouts at the bottom of the stalk and removing the lower leaves as you progress up the stalk. Clearing the mature sprouts and foliage will direct the energy to the developing crop.

**Sow root crop seeds thickly, then thin the plants**   Plant root crop seeds according to label directions, then thin at least twice during the growing season to space the plants evenly and give the roots room to develop. Since the foliage develops in proportion to the size of the root, thin when the foliage is crowded. Allow the plants to develop, then thin a second time when the foliage becomes crowded again. When the tops have room to spread, the roots should have sufficient room, too. Continue making room for the roots to develop by pulling (and eating) a few of the young root plants periodically throughout the growing period.

**Treat infested soils**   If wireworms, cutworms, or root maggots are present in the soil, treat it with diazinon or chlorpyrifos, following label directions.

**Plant one row of onions for scallions, another row for slicers**   Though bunching onions are the best kind for salad and table use, most onion varieties may be used as scallions if picked when they are just developing. Plant a separate row for table use; pulling thinnings from the main onion bed during the season can damage the remaining developing onions.

**Let onion tops shrivel before harvesting**   If the tops take too long to die back, break them with a rake. Wait a week, then dig up the onions. Allow the bulbs to cure in the sunlight or spread them on a dry, paved surface until

*Harvest broccoli heads before they form flowers. They are at their best before the head begins to loosen. More heads will develop after the first is cut.*

the tops have completely shriveled. Cut the stems to 1 inch before storing.

**Allow vegetables to overwinter in the ground** In regions where the soil does not freeze solid during the winter, many vegetables can be left in the ground. Pull them all winter, or make an early spring harvest. Most root crops store this way, but harvest the last ones before the weather warms in the spring; warm weather will cause them to bolt, spoiling the root. Leeks, garlic, and onions can also be pulled all winter. Leeks are very hardy, and can be stored in the ground even in areas where the ground freezes. Brussels sprouts and kale both taste better if harvested after a few good freezes.

**Plant vining peas and beans in double rows** Planted in double rows, vining peas and beans are easily supported. Run a 2- to 4-foot width of fiber or plastic mesh along the center of the path between the two rows. Suspend the mesh vertically, tying it to the upper section of sticks or bamboo poles with plastic or string ties. Sink the ends of the poles into the soil deeply enough to support the weight of the mesh and the vines that will cover it. Guide the developing vines toward the mesh; once they touch it they will grow upward along it. The vines from one row help to balance the weight of the opposite row. The peas or beans will be suspended for easy picking.

**Place black plastic over bean rows** Lay a strip of plastic over a row of freshly sown bean seeds and leave it there for three days to warm the soil evenly and ensure even germination.

**Combine sunflowers and pole beans** The rough texture of sunflower stems will help support bean vines. When the sunflowers reach 2 feet tall, tie them loosely together in twos. Plant the pole beans in a circle around the base of the sunflowers. This is an old tip; Native Americans taught it to European settlers.

**Pick all mature green beans** Leaving even one or two mature beans on the plant will prevent new ones from forming.

**Plant melons and squash in beds with walkways alongside** Spread a heavy layer of mulch on the walkways between planting beds to discourage the vines from encroaching and to make harvesting easier where the ground is muddy.

**Use hot caps for melons and squash** Until the vines begin to run, protect the tender tips from wind and cold by placing hot caps over them. Anchor the hot caps with rocks or mound soil around the bases. Cut a slit in each cap on the side away from prevailing winds to allow air ventilation in case temperatures warm suddenly.

**Harvest muskmelon** Ripe muskmelons give off a strong aroma. Check for maturity by tugging gently on the stem. Ripe melons slip off easily. If the stem resists picking, wait a day or two and try again.

**Harvest honeydew** Ripe honeydews turn cream colored; they feel velvety rather than smooth. Thump lightly; a dull sound signals ripeness.

*Check the ripeness of muskmelons by tugging gently on the stem. Ripe melons will slip off easily.*

**Harvest watermelon**   Ripe watermelons sound hollow and have a rich yellow bottom surface or "ground spot." Knock a watermelon with the knuckles to test for maturity. Green watermelons have a metallic ring.

**Protect cucumbers**   A light covering will shield cucumber plants from cold by night and insects by day. Use cheesecloth, floating row cover, or any other covering that is porous to light and moisture.

**Install a trellis to save space**   In small yards, most vining crops can be trained to a trellis and anchored with soft ties. Make a net or soft cloth sling to support heavy fruit.

**Cut vine borers out of the stems**   Fight back if vine borers have already invaded. Slit the stem with a sharp knife or razor blade to kill the worm. Bury the cut section beneath a layer of soil to encourage rooting along the stem.

*Provide some shade during the hottest part of summer. Lettuce and other greens taste better in hot weather if given some protection from the sun. This garden uses PVC irrigation pipe for frames.*

*This garden incorporates several of the tips mentioned in this chapter: raised beds, a floating row cover, and both plastic and organic mulches.*

**Plant leafy vegetables in rich soils**  To be crisp, greens must be grown quickly, and only rich soils can sustain the rapid growth. Since the root systems of leafy vegetables are shallow, make nutrients available near the soil surface by top-dressing with a complete fertilizer. Place the fertilizer on either side of the row, from the stem to just beyond the spread of the growing leaves.

**Trim greens to extend harvest**  To keep greens producing, start cutting a few outer leaves when growth reaches about 3 inches. If the plant becomes leggy, snip it off at ground level to force new shoots to develop.

**Provide shade to reduce bolting**  In hot weather erect a burlap or landscape fabric shade over leafy vegetables. A fabric shading, 6 to 8 inches above the row, keeps plants cooler and may allow season-long harvests.

**Force insects from harvested greens**  Insects can hide easily in the leaves and tight centers of leafy crops. Washing with water alone may not remove them. Swish harvested greens through salted water to irritate the insects, driving them to the foliage surface, where you can easily wash them away.

**Use hot caps for frost protection**  Position hot caps over the tops of tender plants. Anchor hot caps in place with stones or by mounding soil around the bases. Cut a slash in each hot cap, on the side facing away from prevailing winds. If temperatures rise suddenly, drape a fabric covering over the hot caps to stop the plants from overheating.

**Plant a series of short-season vegetables**  Make short rows of the fast-growing vegetable crops. Harvest them at their prime and immediately plant the next crop in the same spot. Replace the first crop with more of the same, such as radishes after radishes, or lettuce following lettuce. Alternatively, plant different crops, such as early sweet corn followed by turnips, or peppers after radishes.

**Double up crops**  Sow two crops with different growth cycles in the same spot at the same time. For example, place carrot or beet seeds and radish seeds in the same row. The radishes

## Glossary of Fruit and Vegetable Terms

**Bolt**  The process of forming seeds prematurely, usually in reaction to unfavorable growing conditions, such as excessive heat.

**Cross-pollination**  The transfer of pollen from the anther of one flower to the stigma of another with a different genetic composition. Cross-pollination occurs by action of the wind, insects, or deliberately by the gardener.

**Fire blight**  A disease of apple and pear trees that causes new shoots to wither and turn black as if scorched.

**Fruit picker**  A device, usually on a long handle, for picking fruit from trees. A claw extension removes the fruit, and a basket base catches it.

**Fungicide**  Any material that attacks fungi or their spores.

**Hot cap**  A product made of thin, coated paper that is placed over tender plants to protect them from frosts, winds, and hot sun.

**Self-pollination**  The transfer of pollen from an anther to a stigma in the same flower, or to a stigma of another flower on the same plant, or to a stigma of a flower on a plant of the same cultivar.

**Silk**  The silky material produced at the end and inside the husk of an ear of corn.

**Sunscald**  Damage done by the heat of the sun to apple and some other fruits.

**Tassel**  The terminal flower, or inflorescence, at the top of some plants, especially corn plants.

will be ready for harvest before the carrots or beets show much growth.

**Intermix companion crops**  Grow close to each other two or more types of vegetables whose individual characteristics work to the advantage of the other plant. For example, plant tomatoes next to lettuce. Tomatoes are deep rooted and need full sun. They provide beneficial shade to the lettuce. Lettuce has shallow roots that are no competition to the tomato roots, and the lettuce will keep down the weeds that might otherwise grow between the tomato plants.

**Turn the garden into a series of raised beds**  Form raised beds by enclosing an area on all sides with planks or railroad ties and filling it with soil. Staple copper strips to the sides to keep slugs and snails out. Construct permanent pathways between the raised beds for easy access and to keep weeds from growing. Fill each bed with one or more varieties of vegetables, planted closely. Use trellises to support vining crops.

Crops can be produced in one fifth the normal space by using raised beds with good soil and by following companion planting and crop rotation techniques.

## Mail-Order Sources

Try these sources for products not available in your local garden center.

**Gardens Alive!**
Highway 48, Box 149
Sunman, IN 47041
812-623-3800
*Environmentally responsible gardening products.*

**The Natural Gardening Company**
217 San Anselmo Avenue
San Anselmo, CA 94960
415-456-5060
*Copper strips for slug and snail deterrence and many other items.*

**Smith and Hawken**
25 Corte Madera
Mill Valley, CA 94941
415-383-4050
*Gardening tools and equipment.*

**The Urban Farmer**
2833 Vicente Street
San Francisco, CA 94116
*Gardening equipment, including drip irrigation supplies.*

**Wildflower Seed Company**
Box 406
St. Helena, CA 94574
*Variety of wildflower mixes for each region of the United States.*

## Books for Further Reading

Better Homes and Gardens. *Step by Step Landscaping.* Des Moines, Iowa: Meredith Corp., 1991.

Buscher, Fred K., and Susan A. McClure. *All About Pruning.* San Ramon, Calif.: Ortho Information Services, 1989.

Heriteau, Jacqueline, with Dr. H. Marc Cathey, Director, and the staff and consultants of the U.S. National Arboretum. *The National Arboretum Book of Outstanding Garden Plants.* New York: Simon & Schuster, Inc., 1990.

Horton, Alvin, and Lin Cotton. *All About Landscaping.* San Ramon, Calif.: Ortho Information Services, 1988.

Meyers, L. Donald. *The Complete Backyard Planner.* New York: Charles Scribner's Sons, 1985.

Murray, Elizabeth, and Derek Fell. *Home Landscaping: Ideas, Styles, and Designs for Creative Outdoor Spaces.* New York: Simon & Schuster, Inc., 1988.

Ogden, Shepherd and Ellen. *The Cook's Garden: Growing and Using the Best-Tasting Vegetable Varieties.* Emmaus, Penn.: Rodale Press, 1989.

Smith, Michael D., ed. *The Ortho Problem Solver,* 4th ed. San Ramon, Calif.: Ortho Information Services, 1994.

Thomson, Bob, with James Tabor. *The New Victory Garden.* Boston: Little, Brown & Co., 1987.

Vengris, Jonas, and William A. Torello. *Lawns: Basic Factors, Construction and Maintenance of Fine Turf Areas.* 3rd ed. Fresno, Calif.: Thomson Publications, 1982.

Williams, Greg. *The Garden That Cares for Itself.* San Ramon, Calif.: Ortho Information Services, 1990.

## U.S. Measure and Metric Measure Conversion Chart

| | | Formulas for Exact Measures | | | Rounded Measures for Quick Reference | | |
|---|---|---|---|---|---|---|---|
| | Symbol | When you know: | Multiply by: | To find: | | | |
| Mass (weight) | oz | ounces | 28.35 | grams | 1 oz | | = 30 g |
| | lb | pounds | 0.45 | kilograms | 4 oz | | = 115 g |
| | g | grams | 0.035 | ounces | 8 oz | | = 225 g |
| | kg | kilograms | 2.2 | pounds | 16 oz | = 1 lb | = 450 g |
| | | | | | 32 oz | = 2 lb | = 900 g |
| | | | | | 36 oz | = 2¼ lb | = 1000 g (1 kg) |
| Volume | pt | pints | 0.47 | liters | 1 c | = 8 oz | = 250 ml |
| | qt | quarts | 0.95 | liters | 2 c (1 pt) | = 16 oz | = 500 ml |
| | gal | gallons | 3.785 | liters | 4 c (1 qt) | = 32 oz | = 1 liter |
| | ml | milliliters | 0.034 | fluid ounces | 4 qt (1 gal) | = 128 oz | = 3¾ liter |
| Length | in. | inches | 2.54 | centimeters | ⅜ in. | | = 1.0 cm |
| | ft | feet | 30.48 | centimeters | 1 in. | | = 2.5 cm |
| | yd | yards | 0.9144 | meters | 2 in. | | = 5.0 cm |
| | mi | miles | 1.609 | kilometers | 2½ in. | | = 6.5 cm |
| | km | kilometers | 0.621 | miles | 12 in. (1 ft) | | = 30.0 cm |
| | m | meters | 1.094 | yards | 1 yd | | = 90.0 cm |
| | cm | centimeters | 0.39 | inches | 100 ft | | = 30.0 m |
| | | | | | 1 mi | | = 1.6 km |
| Temperature | °F | Fahrenheit | ⅝ (after subtracting 32) | Celsius | 32° F | | = 0° C |
| | °C | Celsius | ⅝ (then add 32) | Fahrenheit | 212° F | | = 100° C |
| Area | in.² | square inches | 6.452 | square centimeters | 1 in.² | | = 6.5 cm² |
| | ft² | square feet | 929.0 | square centimeters | 1 ft² | | = 930 cm² |
| | yd² | square yards | 8361.0 | square centimeters | 1 yd² | | = 8360 cm² |
| | a. | acres | 0.4047 | hectares | 1 a. | | = 4050 m² |

Flower production, increasing, 70, **71**
Foliage, protecting from water, **75**
Foliage-stripped trees, **30**
Folk art, 17
Foresters, government, **6**, 23
Forsythia, 68
Fountains, 17
Frost pockets, 20
Frost protection
  for fruit trees, **79–80**, *80*
  for plants, **72**
  for trees, **33**
  for vegetables, **91**
Fruit growers, commercial, **8–9**, *8*, 77
Fruit pickers, 91
Fruit plants (small)
  grapes and berries, **82–83**, *82, 83*
  terminology for, 91
Fruit trees, *78*, **78–82**, *80, 81*
  *See also specific fruits*
  disease control for, **82**, 91
  fertilizing, **78–79**
  harvesting, **81**, 82
  insect control for, **80–82**
  pollinating, **78**
  protecting, **79–82**, *80*
  pruning, **79**, 82
  spraying, **80**
  terminology for, 91
  watering, **78**
  wrapping, **80**
Fungi
  controlling, *74*, **75**, 82, 91
  and damaged trees, 31, 32
  damping off from, **65**
  and disinfecting tools, 31
  in fruit trees, 82
  heartrot, 32
  in turf, 49
Fungicides, 49, 75, 82, 91

**G**
Garden design. *See* Designing; Planning
Garden ornaments, 17
Gardens Alive!, 92
Garlic, **86**, 89
Gel, germinating seeds in, **65–66**
Germination, **64**, 65–66
Girdling roots, **33**, 56
Gladiolus bulbs, 62, *62*
Glossary
  fruit terms, 91
  landscape design terms, 20
  lawn terms, 53
  nursery terms, 75
  tree terms, 33
  vegetable terms, 91
Glyphosate, 36, 45, 46
Grafting, 75, 78
Grapefruit trees. *See* Citrus trees
Grapes, protecting from birds and bees, **82–83**
Grass. *See* Turf

Green-colored plants, 16–17
Greens, 89, *90*, **91**
Ground covers
  as barriers, 20
  for erosion control, **21**
  planting, **71**
  pruning, 69, **71**, *71*
  rejuvenating, **71**, *71*
  spacing, 71
  around trees, 33
  uses for, 63
Grouping plants, **16**
Growth, allowing for, 16

**H**
Hail, tree damage from, **30**
Hanging containers, 19
Hardening off, **65**
Harvesting fruit, **81**, 82
Heartrot fungi, 32
Hedges
  as barriers, 20
  double-duty, 20
  pruning, **70**
  renewing overgrown, **70**
  as screening, 20
  spacing for, 20
Herbaceous plants, defined, 75
Herb gardens, 17
Herbicides, **36, 37, 45–46**
  preemergence, **46**, 50, **72**
Honeydew melons, **89**
Horticultural professionals, **6–9**, *6–9*, 11, 23, 30
Hot caps, 89, 91
Houseplants, propagating, **68–69**
Humidity, for seedlings, 65
*Hypericum*, pruning, *71*

**I, J**
Ice, protecting trees from, **33**. *See also* Frost protection
Insects
  *See also specific insects*
  controlling, **73–74**, *74*, 80–82, 84–85, 88, 90
  and disinfecting tools, 31, **64**, 67
  in fruit trees, **80–82**
  identifying, **73**
  trapping, **80**
  and tree damage, 31, 32, 33
  in turf, 47, **48–49**
  in vegetables, **84–85**, 88, 90, 91
Invasive plants, **17**, 61, 75
Iris, 67
Irrigation. *See* Drip irrigation; Watering
Ivy, pruning, 69

**K, L**
Kale, 89
Landscape architects, **6**, *6*, 11
Landscape designers, **6**, 11
Landscape designing. *See* Designing
Landscape fabric shields, **72**, 79, 91

Landscape planning. *See* Planning
Lavender-colored plants, 17
Lawn mowers. *See* Mowers
Lawns. *See* Turf
Lawn sprinklers. *See* Sprinklers
Layering, **67–68**, *67*, 75
Layout. *See* Designing; Planning
Leaders, **30**, *30*, 33
Leaf scorching, 24
Leafy vegetables, 89, *90*, **91**
Leaves, protecting from water, **75**
Leave-stripped trees, **30**
Leeks, 89
Lemon trees. *See* Citrus trees
Lettuce, *90*, 91
Lighting
  and designing landscapes, **19**
  and germination, 64
  seedlings, 65
Lilacs, 63, 68
Lilies, 60, 67
Lime, 72
Low-maintenance plants, 16

**M**
Maggots, 80, 88
Mail-order sources, 92
Maintenance, minimizing, 16
Materials lists, 15, **19–20**
Measuring
  metric conversion chart, 92
  sites, **12–13**, *13*, 20
  sprinkler water patterns, **51–52**, *51*
Melons, 85, **89–90**, *89*
Metric conversion chart, 92
Mice, preventing damage by, 62, **73**
Microclimates, 13, 20
Mildew, powdery, 75
Misting, foliage-stripped trees, 30
Mites, 74
Modules, design, **14**
Moisture testing, soil, 24, 51
Moths, coddling, 80
Moving plants. *See* Transplants
Mower blight, **32**
Mowers, **32**, 33
Mowing
  ground covers, **71**, *71*
  turf (mature), 45, 46, **47**, 52
  turf (young), **39–40, 42–43**
  weeds, **44**
Mulching
  berries, **82**
  defined, 53
  ground covers, 71
  new plantings, **59**, 72
  plant debris as mulch, 75
  trees, **33**
  turf, **38–39, 44**, 45
  vegetables, **85**, *90*
  wildflowers, 60
  in winter, **73**
Muskmelons, **89**, *89*

**N**
Natural Gardening Company, The, 92
Nectarine trees, 79
Nitrogen, 50
Nursery plants. *See* Plants
Nursery professionals, **6–8**, *9*, 55
Nursery terms, 75
Nutrients. *See* Fertilizing

**O**
Onions, **88–89**
Orange-colored plants, 17
Orange trees. *See* Citrus trees
Organic amendments, 36, 58
Ornamental grasses, 63
Ornaments, 17
Overgrown shrubs, **70**
Overlays, for planning, **12–13**, 14
Overseeding warm-season grasses, **45**
Overwintering vegetables in ground, **89**

**P, Q**
Padded ties, 29, *29*
Pastel colors, 17
Patching turf, **53**
Pathways. *See* Walkways
Patios
  container plants for, *18*, 19
  and designing landscapes, *16–17*
Peach trees
  fertilizing, 79
  harvesting, 81
  insect control for, 80–82
  pruning, 79
Pear trees
  fertilizing, 78
  fire blight in, 91
  harvesting, 81
  pruning, 79
Peas, **89**
Peat moss, damping off controlled by, **65**
Peonies, 60, 67
Peppers, **86–87**, 91
Perennials
  planting, 60–61, *60*, 63, *63*
  propagating, 66–67, 68–69
  pruning, **69–71**, *70–71*
Pesticides, 74, *74*
Pests. *See* Animals; Insects
pH, soil, **72**
Pheromone traps, 80
Phosphorus, 50
Photocopying plans, **12**
Pine candles, **26**, *26*, 33
Pines, pruning, **26**, *26*
Planning, **11–21**
  base plans, **12–15**, 19, 20
  bubble plans, 14, *14*
  and budget calculation, 15, **20**
  and building codes, **15**
  and cost estimates, 15, 20